THE PIANO

A Pictorial Account of
Its Ancestry and Development

Birthday Greetings to Moravian Bishop van Vleck.
Painting, anonymous, USA, 1795 (Moravian Historical Society, Nazareth, Pennsylvania). This Moravian group is gathered around a stringed keyboard instrument drawn out of scale and appearing gigantic. The unskilled artist omitted important details but a clavichord was surely intended.

Ambrose Andrews Schuyler Family. Painting by an unknown American artist, c. 1824 (The New-York Historical Society). This portrait of an American family, the work of an unschooled painter, shows them seated around their square piano. The piano is painted as carefully as the members of the family, the bottom key correctly shown as FF which it would typically have been at this time. The artist, however, planned his space poorly and was unable to show the top note as f³ although the total length of the keyboard is roughly equivalent to the expected five octaves, judging from the space allotted to the lowest octave. The prominence given to the piano in the composition suggests it was a family treasure.

THE PIANO

A PICTORIAL ACCOUNT OF
ITS ANCESTRY AND DEVELOPMENT

HELEN RICE HOLLIS

A New and Revised Edition

HIPPOCRENE BOOKS
New York

To Anne and Richard and S.Y.

For information, address: Hippocrene Books, Inc.,
171 Madison Avenue, New York, New York 10016.

Printed in the United States of America

Library of Congress Cataloging in Publication Data

Hollis, Helen R.
The piano.

Rev. and augmented ed.
Bibliography: p. 127
Includes index.
1. Piano—History. 2. Piano—Pictorial works.
I. Title.
ML650.H63   1984   786.2'1'09   82-12119
ISBN 0-88254-711-9

CONTENTS

INTRODUCTION

Two works on the history of the piano are and always will be indispensable to the student of the subject. They are: Rosamond E. M. Harding's *The Piano-forte—Its History Traced to the Great Exhibition of 1851,* and Arthur Loesser's *Men, Women and Pianos* that he called "a social history." It is indeed that and much more, as entertaining as it is informative. It seems, however, to cry out for illustrations and I set out to provide some of these, learning later that Mr. Loesser had selected several hundreds to accompany his book, only to learn that the publishers felt that printing costs of these were prohibitive. Dr. Harding, a true pioneer, laid the groundwork for all future studies. I am indebted to these and many other works, as well as to friends and colleagues so numerous that to attempt to list them all would seem presumptuous and would risk regrettable omissions.

In my own studies I have found it useful to explore the stringed keyboard instruments in use before the advent of the piano as a means of understanding how and why they led instrument makers to the piano.

The illustrations used fall into two categories: musical instruments and works of art in which they are depicted. The first group illustrates milestones in the development of stringed keyboards, including some unsuccessful experiments. The works of art are a valuable source of information on forms of instruments now obsolete, and they tell us much about the kinds of people who played instruments and in what settings and combinations they played them.

Few instruments of the Renaissance have survived, fewer still of the Middle Ages, but they are, on the whole, quite reliably depicted in works of art of those times—in paintings, sculptures, tapestries, or stained glass windows. Whether they are played by saints, angels, allegorical or classical figures, or mere mortals, the artist usually portrays them playing instruments of his own time, the only ones he knew.

Flemish and Dutch paintings of the 17th century provide a rich record of domestic musical life of the period. They are convincing evidence of the importance of music to the prosperous burghers; and the instruments are painted with such attention to details that in a few instances we can even identify with some degree of certainty the probable maker of an instrument (see plates 30 and 31).

If a musical instrument in a work of art cannot be verified by other evidence—a surviving instrument or written document—the artist is suspected of having invented, indulged in fantasy or poorly observed his subject. Whether his approach is symbolic, allegorical or humanistic, his work must be carefully considered before any conclusion or reasonable conjecture can be reached as to its validity as musicological study material.

Direct and indirect antecedents of the piano are included—plucked strings as well as struck strings. The harp and psaltery are early ancestors of the harpsichord since their strings are plucked. The dulcimer whose strings are struck with small mallets or hammers gave instrument makers the idea for the piano. Psalteries and dulcimers, like the piano, have strings stretched above attached soundboards. The harpsichord is, in a sense, a mechanized psaltery as the clavichord and piano are mechanized dulcimers. The first pianos, however, were made by a harpsichord maker attempting to increase the dynamic expressivity of his instrument. Further, since it was the piano that ultimately replaced the harpsichord, the latter must be considered among the instruments leading to the development and ascendancy of the piano, although its strings are plucked rather than struck.

Bartolomeo Cristofori invented the piano shortly before 1700. He was an Italian harpsichord maker and called his new instrument *gravicembalo col piano e forte*—harpsichord with soft and loud. Pianoforte, thus, became and remains its proper name. Although other designations such as forte piano and Hammerklavier (Beethoven's chauvinistic preference) have been tried, the shortened word, piano, is accepted in most languages and is used throughout this book.

The majority of the illustrations were provided by the collections, libraries or museums in which the examples are housed. Exceptions are the following: plates 10, 15, Gabinetto Fotografico Nazionale, Rome; 12, 13, 21, Royal Commission on Historical Monuments, National Monuments Record, London; 22, Perfecta Publications Ltd; 5, 23, 24, 28, 46, Photographie Giraudon, Paris; 25, Lichtbildwerkstätte 'Alpenland', Vienna; 42, Royal Academy of Arts, London; 47, 48, Musée Instrumental du Conservatoire National de Musique, Paris; 56, A. C. Cooper Fine Art Photographer, London; 97, 99, Steinway & Sons; page 65, Victoria & Albert Museum.

I

EARLIEST ANCESTORS

Harps of one kind or another of many sizes and shapes were known in most early civilisations. The addition of a soundboard to a harp produces a psaltery or a dulcimer. These, too, appear in many different forms (plates 1–5).

Keyboards attached to organs made their appearance early in history—Hero of Alexandria described an organ with a keyboard in the third century BC—and the application of a keyboard to a stringed instrument was described as early as the tenth century by St Odo who wrote of the organistrum, a remarkably ingenious instrument in which several strings rest against a resined wheel. The wheel is turned by a crank setting the strings in vibration, much as does the bow on the strings of a violin. Some of the organistrum's strings are unstopped, providing a drone accompaniment to a melody played on a small keyboard of some kind that causes tangents to press against other strings. The tangent mechanism is similar to the simple mechanism of the clavichord and indeed may have suggested it.

In the twelfth century the organistrum is depicted as a large fiddle-shaped instrument that required two people to play—one to turn the wheel and the other to stop the strings. Later types (plates 6, 7) are played by a single person. We know the organistrum today as the hurdy-gurdy.

PLATE I
Angel playing a psaltery. Sculpture in marble by Andrea Orcagna, Italy, c. 1308–68 (The Norton Simon Foundation, Fullerton, California). Here the psaltery appears to be held by a band around the angel's shoulders as he plucks the strings with the index finger of the left hand while the right hand uses a long quill as a plectrum. The psaltery is sometimes held with one hand while the other plays. Elsewhere one sees it held on the lap or set on a table leaving both hands free to play.

PLATE 2

Madonna and child in a closed garden. Colored woodcut, anonymous German, Swabian or Franconian, c. 1450–70 (National Gallery of Art, Washington, DC, Rosenwald Collection). The angel (right) plucks the strings of the psaltery with several fingers of each hand while supporting the instrument by resting its in-curved sides on the crooks of his bent elbows.

PLATE 5

Dulcimer player, page from an illuminated manuscript entitled *Le livre des échecs amoureux*, France, sixteenth century Bibliothèque Nationale, Paris, ms fr 143. The lady is holding two light crook-shaped hammers for striking the strings. Psalteries and dulcimers appear in a variety of shapes, but the details are usually indistinguishable except for the manner in which they are played. When the strings are plucked the instrument is a psaltery; when they are struck it is a dulcimer. Musicians in the background play pipe and tabor, shawm, and bagpipes, and sing from a manuscript. A small harp, a portative organ, and a recorder rest on the floor. The dulcimer survives today as a folk instrument in many countries. In Rumania and Hungary it is *cimbalom,* in Iran *santur,* in Greece *santouri.* It is found in America in scattered communities of European origin where folk practices of the mother country are still remembered.

PLATE 6 *(above left)*
Angel with an organistrum. Sculpture in marble by Andrea Orcagna, Italy, c. 1308–64 (National Gallery of Art, Washington, DC, Samuel H. Kress Collection). Hero of Alexandria described a hydraulic organ with a keyboard, in the third century BC, but the organistrum is the earliest form of a stringed instrument provided with a keyboard. It is described by Saint Odo of Cluny in the tenth century and depicted as early as the twelfth century as a large fiddle-shaped instrument that required two people to play—one to turn the wheel and one to stop the strings.

The crank turns a resined wheel which presses against the strings setting them in vibration. The tangents operated by the keys then stop the strings, as do a violinist's fingers, to play a melody. In this sculpture the keys are round buttons played with one hand while the other hand turns the wheel—a one-person operation which became standard. The tangent mechanism is similar to the simple mechanism of the clavichord and indeed may have suggested it. Today we call an instrument working on the same principle, a "hurdy-gurdy."

2

CLAVICHORDS

The clavichord was derived from the application of a keyboard to the monochord—a mathematical more than a musical instrument that was used by Greek philosophers, notably Pythagoras, for investigating the nature of musical sound. In the eleventh century, Guido of Arezzo employed the monochord to indicate the eight tones of the ecclesiastical modes on which the plainsong of the Church was based.

The terms monochord, manichordion, and manichord seem early to have been used interchangeably to denote the device described above or the instrument we now call 'clavichord', a word which first appeared in 1404 in the rules for the Minnesingers.

The mechanism of the clavichord is of the utmost simplicity. Each key has an upright metal tangent attached to its rear end; when a key is depressed its tangent strikes metal strings—usually a pair for each note. Felt strips are threaded between the strings at their left ends to prevent that portion from vibrating; the sounding lengths of the strings (ie the pitch determinants) are the distances between the points at which the tangents touch them and the bridge at the right.

Since the tangent remains in contact with the strings as long as the key is held down the sound produced is very small, but the clavichord is peculiarly touch sensitive and is capable of gradation of dynamics within a small range and of a delicate vibrato *(Bebung)*. The latter is an effect unique among keyboard instruments and is possible because the performer may vary the pressure of the key he is holding down, thereby varying the pressure of the tangent on the strings to cause a subtle fluctuation of pitch as well as to prolong the vibration (plate 8).

The small sound and subtle expression of the clavichord preclude its use as an ensemble or accompanying instrument. It is an instrument to play for one's solitary pleasure or for friends in an intimate setting (plates 16, 17).

It is not known or likely to be known just where the first clavichords were made but descriptions suggesting some sort of stringed keyboard instrument exist in Burgundian, French, English and Spanish writings as early as the fourteenth century. Makers of harpsichords are known to have been working in Italy as early as 1419. Indications from works of art are clear, however, that by the mid-fifteenth century, clavichords and harpsichords were rather widely known on the European continent[2] as well as the British Isles. The variety of media of these representations is as striking as their widespread provenances (plates 9–14).

The early representations of clavichords show instruments, the strings

Fig. 1
A woodcut of a mono-chord in *Musica Theorica* by Lodovico Fogliano, published in Venice in 1529

of which are in unison and on which no soundboard is visible. There has been speculation as to whether a soundboard may have run under the keys and indeed the presence of a soundboard is indicated in a drawing in Henri Arnault's remarkable fifteenth-century treatise on musical instruments (plate 11) and in his notes which speak of the upper and lower bottoms. A painting by a follower of the 'Master of the Half Lengths' (plate 17) shows a clavichord with a soundboard clearly visible under the keys.

The earliest clavichords were fretted *(gebunden),* ie one pair of strings served for several keys (plate 18a). Only at a later date were clavichords made in which two or even three strings were provided for each key—unfretted *(bundfrei)* (plate 18b).

Toward the end of the fifteenth century, strings tuned to different pitches began to appear on clavichords (plate 15) and ultimately the instrument was lengthened to accommodate a larger soundboard at the right end.

PLATE 8
Model of clavichord action (Smithsonian Institution). The middle tangent on the end of the key that is being depressed is striking its pair of strings.

Altarpiece from cathedral *(right)* from the cathedral at Minden, Germany, 1425 (Bodemuseum, Berlin, German Democratic Republic). The earliest representation of the clavichord and harpsichord at present known are seen in this sculpture in the section of the border just below right center. No explanation is offered for the bass strings being on the wrong side of the harpsichord either in this or the Kefermarkt sculpture in plate 25.

PLATE 10
Fresco by Leonardo da Besozzo, Naples, c. 1428[3] (Caracciolo Chapel of San Giovanni a Carbonara, Naples, Italy). The primitive clavichord here (accompanied by psaltery and bells) has no visible soundboard.

PLATE 11
Portion of a page from the treatise on musical instruments by Henri Arnault de Zwolle, c. 1440 (Bibliothèque Nationale, Paris, ms fonds Latin 7295). This page shows the layout of a clavichord. Arnault gives directions for determining the sounding lengths of the strings. As with other clavichords of early date, the strings are tuned in unison and the soundboard, a part of which is visible, may extend beneath the keys as Arnault's notes seem to indicate.

PLATE 12
Clavichord represented in stained glass window designed by John Prudde, commissioned 1441 (St Mary's Church, Warwick, England).

PLATE 13
Angel playing a clavichord. Sculpture in wood, before 1471. (Church of St Mary, Shrewsbury, England). This crude sculpture is an attempt to represent a fretted clavichord. More keys than strings are indicated.

PLATE 14

Page from *Weimarer Ingenieurkunst und Wunderbuch (Weimar Engineering Art and Miracle Book)* (Thuringische Landesbibliothek, Weimar, Germany, ms fol 328). This naive drawing of a harpsichord and clavichord is shown as much for the questions it raises as for the information it furnishes. It is often reproduced and has been dated c. 1440. According to Konrad Marwinski, Chief of the Department of Information and Special Collections, Weimar Library, this date is in doubt; he finds that the manuscript is the work of several hands, that the style of clothing points to the first half of the sixteenth century and that there appears in the manuscript a portrait of Maximilian I (1459–1519). He adds, however, that the 1440 date has some relevance in that many of the drawings in the codex are copies of others done some 100 years earlier.[4] The exact date, then, remains conjectural.

The illustrator has neglected to show bridges or mechanisms for the instruments and has drawn keyboards with each narrow key set between a pair of wider ones—an unlikely arrangement even for an early diatonic keyboard. Obviously, the instruments as shown could not function, but the same keyboard plan is said to be visible in a manuscript preserved in the public library of Ghent, Belgium, and believed to date from the fourteenth century.

PLATE 15

Clavichord by Johann Adolf Hass, Hamburg, 1756. Compass C to d, double and triple (15 lowest notes) strung fretted. (Smithsonian Institution 1980.0020.01)

View of painted soundboard and stringing.

PLATE 16
Woman playing a clavichord. Painting attributed to Jan van Hemessen, Flemish, 1500–66 (Worcester Art Museum, Worcester, Massachusetts). This charming scene gives an excellent impression of the intimacy associated with the clavichord. Its tone is so delicate that it is ideal only for solitary musical self-communion, or to be played for a small group in an intimate setting.

PLATE 17
Woman with a clavichord. Painting by a follower of the Master of the Female Half-lengths, Flemish, c. 1535–40 (Collection of Adelyn D. Breeskin, Washington, DC). Here one sees how easily a small clavichord could be moved around to be put on a table or stand for use. A soundboard is visible beneath the keys.

PLATES 18a and 18b

Plan views of two clavichords. *(Top)* Germany, eighteenth century (Smithsonian Institution, 60,1394, formerly Cooper Union Collection); *(bottom)* by Johann Michael Voit, Schweinfurth, Germany, 1812 (Smithsonian Institution, 303,542, Hugo Worch Collection). These two views show the arrangements of the keys of a fretted and an unfretted clavichord. They also show the change from the earlier examples which have unison strings of equal lengths and soundboards extending under the keys, to a design with strings graduated in length and gauge and a more effective soundboard raised at the right end.

The upper instrument is fretted, which accounts for the angling of the rear of the keys; the seemingly erratic spacing is necessary because some pairs of keys must strike the same pairs of strings. The lower instrument is unfretted—each key has its own pair of strings. It was a large unfretted clavichord on which Carl Phillip Emmanuel Bach's playing deeply moved his contemporaries. In earlier examples as many as four keys struck the same pair of strings.

24

3

HARPSICHORDS

The harpsichord, virginal and spinet[6] make their music by plucking metal strings from a keyboard. An upright jack of wood equipped with a plectrum in a pivoted tongue rests on the rear end of each key. When a key is depressed the jack travels up and the plectrum plucks a string en route. With the release of the key the jack falls and the plectrum, thanks to the pivoted tongue, barely touches the string without any audible sound on its way back down. Each jack has its own small felt damper that rests on the string until the key is struck and lifts as the string is plucked to permit its vibration as long as the key is held down.

A wooden bar is suspended from the sides of the frame above the jacks to prevent their jumping up out of place. The underside of this jack-rail is cushioned with felt to deaden the noise of the jacks hitting against it (plate 19).

One or several strings are played from one or two (in rare examples, three) keyboards, this variation made possible by stops or other arrangements to shift the jacks from playing to non-playing position. The plectra are most often of crow quill, but sometimes of cowhide or buffalo skin.

The harpsichord speaks with a clarity that makes it ideally suitable for delineating parts in a polyphonic texture or for playing a chordal accompaniment to a melody. While graded dynamics are impossible to achieve by varying the pressure on the keys, this may be accomplished by the structure of the music itself. The great harpsichord-composers cannily built up or diminished the volume of sound by altering the spacing of the parts, or by adding or subtracting notes to thicken or thin the texture. In performance a note may be emphasized by ornamenting it with a trill or a turn, or prolonged by repeating it or extending the trill.

The rich sonority of the harpsichord is fully revealed by the composers of its solo literature. For the terrace dynamics or echo effects of some Baroque music, the instrument with two keyboards and several sets of strings is especially suitable. Such a harpsichord characteristically has two sets of strings at 'normal' (ie 8') pitch and one set tuned an octave higher (4'). (Only rarely does it have a set at 16' or one at 2' pitch (one octave below, or two above, normal pitch).[7]

An elusive keyboard instrument, the *échiquier*,[8] existed along with the clavichord and harpsichord in the sixteenth century. The word seems not to have been simply another name for one of these, since *échiquier* and *épinette* (harpsichord) appear together in sixteenth-century documents. The *échiquier* is mentioned also as an accompaniment to dancing for which the sound of a clavichord is too delicate.

It is possibly the instrument described by Henri Arnault in the last of his four plans for making a clavisymbalom, as follows:

> This key has a piece attached to its upper part and leaded so that when the key is struck and strikes against an obstacle above near the strings this piece is projected in the direction of the strings, and, after having touched them, falls back, given that the key is held down.[9]

This is remarkably suggestive of the escapement of the piano action and tantalizing since no such instrument or representation of it is known to have survived. One of the terms used for it is *eschaquier d' Angleterre,* inviting the conjecture that it may have originated or was especially popular in England.

As mentioned previously, the earliest depiction of a harpsichord now known dates from 1425 (plate 9) and the manuscript of Henri Arnault (plate 20) c. 1440 not only gives a layout of a harpsichord but also describes four possible ways of constructing the plucking mechanism.

The harpsichord was to assume a number of sizes and shapes and to acquire some sophisticated refinements. The larger instruments were played in palaces and great houses, in concert, theatre and church performances, the spinets and virginals in domestic settings. In art one sees it in both angelic and earthly settings (plates 21–50).

PLATE 19

Model of harpsichord action (detail) (Smithsonian Institution). This shows jack-slides from which some jacks have been removed. The plectrum of the jack on the left in front is about to pluck the string as the key on which it stands is depressed. The jack behind this has its plectrum pointing in the other direction and only the rear end of it can be seen. The other jacks are at rest, their felt dampers sitting on the strings. Above can be seen a section of the jack-rail with its felt padding.

PLATE 20

Page from the treatise on musical instruments by Arnault de Zwolle c.1440 (Bibliothèque Nationale, Paris, ms fonds Latin 7295). On this page Arnault shows the layout of a wing-shaped keyboard instrument accompanied by detailed drawings of jacks, and gives instructions for four methods of constructing a clavisymbalom. The treatise is in 'dog Latin', full of abbreviations and difficult to read, but the systems, as well as they can be understood, seem workable, although at least one of them is highly cumbersome. In one plan the strings are struck rather than plucked (see the description of the fourth plan on p 26), indicating that Arnault was using the word clavisymbalom to include more than one type of stringed keyboard instrument. The French translators of the manuscript[10] found evidence that Arnault was describing instruments actually in existence during his time rather than theorizing about how one might make a musical instrument. With his plan for a clavichord (plate 11), these are among the earliest-known representations of the 'modern' form of the keyboard with accidentals in twos and threes.

The exact date that the chromatic keyboard came into use is unknown, but it is seen as early as c.1426 on an organ played by St Cecilia in a painting by Hubert and Jan van Eyck in St Bavon Cathedral, Ghent.

PLATE 25
Sculpture 1490-8 (parish church of Kefermarkt, upper Austria). The instrument on the left was once considered to be the earliest known representation of an upright harpsichord or *clavicytherium*. The capital, however, has been restored and it is now believed that the instrument was originally a small or *portatif* organ. It is played by an angel while two others play shawm and lute.

PLATE 26
Clavicytherium; compass C/ E to g³, I × 8′ (Royal College of Music, London, Donaldson Collection).[7] This is said to be the earliest existing upright harpsichord. Believed to date from the last twenty years of the fifteenth

century,[13] it may therefore be the oldest extant stringed keyboard instrument of any type. Instead of the familiar structure of the soundboard, the narrow soundboard is supported by the bentside and an almost parallel inner bentside. A sculptured landscape of softwood suggesting a north Italian style is applied to the back; but a fragment of a lease contracted at Ulm and pasted over a split in the back of the instrument suggests it may have been used and possibly even made in Swabia. The instrument has been exactly copied except for the ornamentation by a fine English harpsichord-builder. The sophisticated action works flawlessly and the tone is sweet and ringing.

PLATE 27

Plan view of a virginal by an unknown Italian maker, Italy, sixteenth or seventeenth century; compass[7] C/E to c[3] (Smithsonian Institution, 303,545, Hugo Worch Collection). The smaller plucked stringed keyboard instruments included the virginals—polygonal or rectangular—operating in the same manner as the harpsichord, but possessing only one set of strings. The virginal shown here is tuned according to a system known as 'short octave' tuning. This was an idea carried over from organ building where it was an economy measure, the long low-pitched pipes being expensive in material and labor.

For most music through the seventeenth century the lowest accidentals were non-essential and were often omitted on keyboard instruments of the time. The most common were the C and the G short octaves. In the former, indicated C/E, the lowest key which appears to be E sounds C, the F♯ key sounds D and the G♯, E. In the G short octave indicated as GG/BB, apparent BB sounds GG, apparent C♯ and D♯ sound AA and BB respectively.

Early virginal music often contains widely spaced chords possible to play only on a short octave instrument.

Fig. 2
Arrangement of keys of
short octave keyboards.

31

PLATE 28 *(above)*

Concert Champêtre, anonymous, Italy, sixteenth century (Musée du Berry, Bourges, France). Here an Italian virginalist is playing *basso continuo*[14] in company with viola da gamba, lute, and recorder. The virginal is remarkably similar to the one in the preceding plate, although, apparently, clumsy repainting has disarranged its keys and obliterated the strings of the lute.

PLATE 29 *(facing page, below)*

Polygonal virginal, Italy, sixteenth century; compass GG/BB to c³ (Victoria and Albert Museum, London, 19–1887). The virginal shown here has long been known as Queen Elizabeth's; on the left panel are the arms borne by Henry IV and successive monarchs until Elizabeth's death in 1603, and on the right the badge, a falcon crowned and holding a sceptre, used by both Anne Boleyn and her daughter. The instrument is unsigned but is certainly of Italian origin, and probably of the late sixteenth century. It is one of the most sumptuous of virginals and worthy of a queen. Its front face is elaborately decorated with arabesques painted in gold on panels of red surrounded by green borders. The inside of the hinged front section of the outer case is built to serve as a music desk—an unusual feature. The inner surface is painted with foliage in gold on a gold-sprinkled black ground. The natural keys are ebony-topped with gilded fronts and the accidentals are inlaid with ivory, silver and various woods. The outer case is covered with crimson velvet and lined with yellow satin.

Her contemporaries reported that Queen Elizabeth played the virginal with both pleasure and competence. The extensive collection of her father, Henry VIII, himself an enthusiastic musician, included an astonishing number of keyboard instruments: virginals, clavichords, regals, claviorgana and an instrument described in the Privy Purse expenses of 1530 as a pair of virginals in one coffer with four stops—an early two-manual harpsichord.

The virginal was called 'virginals' or 'pair of virginals' in the sixteenth century, the word pair being applied to complex musical instruments (ie pair of bagpipes, organs, clavichords, virginals, etc). The origin of the term is a matter for speculation, and several theories are advanced. The most convincing seems to be that it was an instrument thought 'proper for girls' (from the Latin *virginalis*), the lute, considered more difficult to play, being reserved as the 'manly' instrument. I have come across only one painting, Italian, showing a man seated at a virginal, but there are many representations of young women picturesquely standing or (rarely) seated at virginals. Shakespeare commemorates them in his sonnet number 128:

> How oft, when thou, my music play'st,
> Upon that blessed wood whose motion sounds
> With thy sweet fingers, when thou gently sway'st
> The wiry concord that mine ear confounds,
> Do I envy those jacks that nimble leap
> To kiss the tender inward of thy hand,
> Whilst my poor lips, which should that harvest reap,
> At the wood's boldness by thee blushing stand!
> To be so tickled, they would change their state
> And situation with those dancing chips,
> O'er whom thy fingers walk with gentle gait,
> Making dead wood more blest than living lips.
> > Since saucy jacks so happy are in this,
> > Give them thy fingers, me thy lips to kiss.

It seems the poet confused the mechanics of the virginal; the jacks of the instrument can hardly,'nimbly leap to kiss the tender inward of thy hand'.

PLATE 33
Double virginal by Hans Ruckers the Elder, Antwerp, 1581 (Metropolitan Museum of Art, New York). This detail shows the *ottavino* set above the other keyboard as described in the previous caption.

PLATE 34
Claviorganum by Alexander Bertolotti, Venice, 1585 (Les Amis du Musée Instrumental du Conservatoire Royal de Musique, Bruxelles). The claviorganum is an instrument designed for versatility in which a harpsichord or virginal is combined with an organ. The two instruments can be played separately or coupled together. At a later date some pianos were 'organized', the procedure for which was described by Bedos de Celles in *L'Art du facteur d'orgues,* Paris, 1778.[15]

PLATE 35a and 35b
Painting and detail *(below)* by Friedrich von Falckenburg, Germany, 1619 (Germanisches Nationalmuseum, Nürnberg, Germany). This is the painted cover of the virginal that sat on top of an organ to make of it the claviorganum depicted in the picture. Only the cover now survives. The main portion of the painting shows the seasons in landscapes of the four estates of Lucas Friederich Behaim, who owned the instrument. Pictured in the center, a detail of which appears below, are musicians in the midst of autumnal wine-making festivities. They are playing the claviorganum two *viole da gamba,* a violin and a viola. Behaim himself is seen playing bass *viola da gamba* while the house music-master, Johann Staden, plays *basso continuo* on the claviorganum. The maker of the virginal, Paul Wissmayr, is standing to the right of the musicians together with the painter and Stefan Cuntz, the builder of the organ.

37

PLATE 36

Plan view of a virginal by Ionnes Battista Boni, Cortona, Italy, 1617; compass C/E to f³, I × 8′ (Smithsonian Institution, 60,1392, formerly Cooper Union Collection, New York). The system of tuning known as 'equal temperament' that came to be favored over others by the end of the eighteenth century and is now in general use divides the octave into twelve equal semi-tones permitting each accidental to serve for either a sharp or its nearest flat. One can then modulate freely from one key to another.

In other systems in use earlier a shade of difference exists between a sharp and the adjacent flat, and certain chromatic notes satisfactory in some keys are unworkable in others. The enharmonic keyboard shown here is for the purpose of producing this difference for some notes. It has accidentals divided from front to back for $e^b/d\#$, $g\#/a^b$, $e^{b1}/d\#^1$, $g\#^1/a^{b1}$. The front halves of the divided accidentals at the bottom extend the keyboard compass by short octave tuning as described on p31, while the back halves retain the F♯ and G♯ normally missing on short octave keyboards. This is known as 'broken octave' tuning. Many experiments were made with enharmonic compositions and keyboards divided into quarter-tones. Scipione Maffei included in his article of 1711 on Cristofori's piano

MIDDLE C↑

Fig. 3
Arrangement of keys of virginal above

(p52) a description of a 'rare' harpsichord designed to cope with the problem of 'the tuning not being equal in all keys'. He saw it in Florence and described it as having five sets of keys one above the other tuned in such a manner that 'you may modulate and run through all the keys without any dissonance'. The Museo Civico in Bologna has such an instrument. At a later date some pianos were made with divided accidentals for 'unequal' tuning (see p68).

PLATE 37 *(left)*

Plan view of a harpsichord dated 1693 by an unknown Italian maker; compass GG to c³ (no GG♯), I × 8′, two hand stops (Smithsonian Institution, 326,904, Hugo Worch Collection). The Italians were satisfied with a relatively simple harpsichord such as this throughout the Renaissance and Baroque eras. Two sets of 8′ strings answered admirably their requirements which were mainly to accompany other instruments and/or voices. A typical Italian harpsichord of this date is lightly constructed and often provided with a heavier ornamented outer case. It was customary to remove the harpsichord from its case placing it on a table for performance.

The oldest extant harpsichord known was made in 1521 by Jerome of Bologna and is in the Victoria and Albert Museum, London.

PLATE 38

Spinet by Thomas Hitchcock, London, between 1703 and 1710; compass GG to g³, I × 8′ (Smithsonian Institution, 62,382). This is still another form of the small domestic plucked-stringed keyboard instrument with one string for each key (see plates 27, 28, 29). The terminology for these instruments is confused, but several authorities have now agreed to use the term 'virginal' for the rectangular or polygonal instruments which have their keyboards and their strings parallel to the long sides, and 'spinet' for the small, bent side, wing shaped instrument in which the tuning pins are in front above the keyboard and the strings are stretched diagonally.

PLATE 39 *(above left)*

Harpsichord by Johannes Daniel Dulcken, Antwerp, 1745; compass FF to f³, 2 × 8′, 1 × 4′, lute, four hand stops (Smithsonian Institution, 315,758, Hugo Worch Collection). This beautiful instrument is in the fine tradition of harpsichord building established by the Ruckers family. It has two sets of strings at 8′ pitch one playable from both keyboards, the other from the lower, one set of strings at 4′ pitch on the lower, and on the upper a 'lute' stop engaging a set of jacks which pluck close to the nut (ie the bridge on the wrest-plank) to produce a nasal lute-like sound.

The earlier double harpsichords of the Flemings were usually, if not always, transposing instruments, the two manuals arranged so that they played at different pitches, usually a fourth or fifth apart. French seventeenth-century makers are associated with the development of the type of instrument shown here with two keyboards playing at the same pitch. Frank Hubbard calls them the 'expressive double'.[16]

Fig. 4

Drawing of rose in soundboard of Dulcken harpsichord

PLATE 40 *(above right)*

Plan view of the harpsichord by Dulcken shown in the preceding plate. The Flemish and French harpsichord builders decorated the soundboards of their instruments with flowers, butterflies, etc, in delicate tempera colors in the charming manner shown here. The ornamental rosette set into a hole in this soundboard is a free design of gilt metal in which one would expect to find Dulcken's initials. They cannot, however, be clearly discerned, although the inclusion of the maker's initials was a Flemish guild regulation. The roses in Italian harpsichords or virginals are of abstract design and usually made of layers of parchment and gilded. Whatever their design or material, they have no function except as decoration or identification of the maker.

PLATE 41

Harpsichord made by Burkat Shudi in London, c. 1743; compass FF to f³ (no FF♯), 2 × 8', 1 × 4', lute, buff, five hand stops (Smithsonian Institution, 314,524, Hugo Worch Collection). This harpsichord is similar in its disposition to the one by Dulcken shown in Plate 39, ie two sets of 8' and one set of 4' strings, lute stop, and with an added stop (buff, sometimes called harp) which moves small leather pads against one set of 8' strings to produce a muted effect. The simple, handsome case of fine wood (here walnut burl veneer) with brass hardware is typical of the English makers.

Burkat Shudi (originally Burckardt Tschudi) was a Swiss who came to London as a joiner and soon thereafter became apprenticed to Hermann Tabel, a Fleming knowledgeable in the traditions of harpsichord building of his country. Shudi was making instruments under his own name by 1729. In 1761 he took as apprentice a young Scot, John Broadwood, who, eight years later, married Shudi's daughter. Ultimately the name of the firm changed to Shudi and Broadwood and the business continues to this day as the highly respected piano-making firm of John Broadwood and Sons, which is still operated by descendants of the founder.

PLATE 42
Burkat Shudi and his family, unknown painter, England, c. 1745 (copy) (collection of Captain Evelyn Broadwood, Capel, Surrey, England). The famous harpsichord-maker (1702–73) is shown here tuning his own instrument, his wife and two sons nearby. Shudi was prominent in London musical life. Handel frequented his house and possessed one of his harpsichords. The Mozarts, father and son, also knew him and admired his instruments. In 1766 he presented a two-manual harpsichord to Frederick the Great, who ordered two more and sent a ring to the maker.

PLATE 43
The Singing Party. Painting of the English school, mid-eighteenth century (National Gallery of Art, Washington, DC; gift of Duncan Phillips). Although painters rarely depicted men playing virginals, the artist here shows a man performing on a harpsichord that recalls the one by Shudi shown in plate 41. A typical eighteenth-century bassoon playing, it may be assumed, the bass line, while the keyboard plays the harmonic accompaniment from a figured bass.[17]

PLATE 44
Harpsichord by Benoist Stehlin, Paris 1760; compass FF to f³, 2 × 8′, 1 × 4′, buff, shove coupler, two hand stops (Smithsonian Institution, 66,521). This is one of only two known surviving harpsichords by Benoist Stehlin, an emigrant from Alsace to Paris. Like those by Dulcken (plate 39) and Shudi (plate 41), it has two sets of strings at 8′ pitch and one at 4′. The upper manual slides in to couple the two manuals, an arrangement known as 'shove coupler'.

The great names in French harpsichord-making were Pascal Taskin (1723–93) and the Blanchets: Nicholas (d. 1731), François Etienne (c. 1705–61) and François Etienne II (1730–66). Many Flemish harpsichords by members of the Ruckers family and others had been acquired by Frenchmen, and during the first half of the eighteenth century the French makers were adroit at extending their range up to five octaves to make them suitable for performing the music of Couperin, Rameau and others. Many of the Ruckers' instruments were altered in this way, an operation known as *ravalement*. The instruments built by the Blanchets and Taskin are modelled on these rebuilt instruments and are esteemed for their rich and brilliant tone.

Taskin is distinguished for having originated the *peau de buffle* stop—jacks with plectra made of buffalo hide producing sounds rhapsodically described in Diderot's *Encyclopedia* of 1788 as 'delicious and velvety . . . rich, mellow, suave and voluptuous'. He also invented knee levers to facilitate changes of registration.

PLATE 45 *(above)*
Plan view of the harpsichord by Benoist Stehlin in the preceding plate. The rose contains the maker's initials and the date, 1760, is painted in red on the soundboard near the long side above and to the right of the rose.

PLATE 46
Mozart père et ses enfants.
Watercolor by L. C. de Car-
montelle, France, 1763
(Musée de Condé, Chan-
tilly, France). The boy
Mozart, aged seven, at a
French harpsichord with his
father and sister.

PLATE 47 *(facing page)*
Harpsichord by Hieronymus Hass, Hamburg, 1740; compass FF to f³ (no
FF♯), three manuals, five sets of strings 1 × 16', 2 × 8', 1 × 4' and 1 ×
2' (to c¹) (collection of Rafael Puyana, Paris). Although German writers
have left us valuable treatises on the construction of musical instruments
in the sixteenth and seventeenth centuries, surviving stringed keyboard
instruments made in Germany before 1700 are scarce. The eighteenth-
century clavichords and harpsichords are, however, among the finest. The
Germans were especially fond of the clavichord and after rather primitive
examples of the early eighteenth century more elaborate instruments made
by fine craftsmen appeared. Far more clavichords than harpsichords are
known; the former, much less expensive to make, was the keyboard
instrument for most musical households and must have been quite prevalent. The clavichord by Voit made in 1812 (plate 18b) is evidence that the
Germans were the last to give up the clavichord in favor of the piano.

The German harpsichords that have survived—some twenty-nine are
presently known—are unusually elegant and suitable for palaces,
churches, theatres or opera houses. A great many must have been neglected or abandoned when the piano was finally accepted and old styles
and practices gave way for the new.

PLATE 48
Plan view of the harpsichord
by Hieronymus Hass in the
preceding illustration.

The most prominent names among the eighteenth-century makers are Hieronymus Albrecht Hass and his son Johann Adolph. They made no standard instrument and the various dispositions of their harpsichords indicate that each was made to order for its client. The use of 16′ and 2′ stops is extremely rare.

The one in this illustration is a *tour de force* and surely the *chef d'œuvre* of its maker. It might be said to possess an embarrassment of riches since the two-manual harpsichords shown in previous illustrations are fully adequate for the performance of the literature of the great harpsichord composers. The case is painted to simulate tortoise-shell and overlaid with Chinese scenes painted in gold. The picture inside the lid shows the harpsichord being presented to an unidentified lady. (Incidentally, this instrument is depicted on its own case, like the one in plates 35a and 35b.) The natural keys are covered with tortoise shell, the accidentals are ivory with tortoise shell inlay, and the keyboard surround is inlaid with these materials. If the bottom of the three keyboards is not to be used, it can be pushed into the instrument like the drawer of a chest.

45

PLATE 49

Harpsichord by Johann Adolf Hass, Hamburg, 1764; compass FF to f³, 2 × 8', 1 × 4' (Russell Collection, University of Edinburgh). Here is a simple but elegant harpsichord by the son of the maker of the unusually elaborate one in the two preceding plates. The beautiful case-work of mahogany veneer is applied even to the back (ie the long-side or spine). In general, this side, not intended to be seen, is left unfinished. The sound-board has no rose but is decorated with painted flowers. The instrument was restored about 1840 and it is possible that the present keyboard with ivory naturals and ebony accidentals replaced one with these materials reversed as was more usual in German instruments of this date. Documentary evidence indicates that this harpsichord once belonged to Mozart.

4

THE TRANSITION TO PIANO

By the beginning of the seventeenth century, musical trends had been set in motion which were to contribute ultimately to the invention of the piano and its acceptance as a replacement for the harpsichord.

The beginning of the period in music we now call Baroque is conveniently ascribed to the date 1600, and its end to the death of Johann Sebastian Bach in 1750, or, more precisely, that of George Frideric Handel nine years later.

Shortly before 1600 a group of Florentine musical intellectuals, known as the 'Camerata', discussed and speculated upon the nature of classical Greek drama, and specifically the style of musical utterance they believed to be its distinguishing characteristic.

The members of the Camerata voiced their dissatisfaction with the polyphonic music of the Renaissance with its thick layers of melodies interwoven and interdependent as an effective style for the expression of personal, subjective, dramatic and violent feelings. Not content merely to complain, several of their members wrote experimental operas. *'Daphne'* by Jacopo Peri, first performed in 1597, and his *'Euridice'*, in 1600, are considered the first operas worthy of the name from both the musical and literary points of view. They introduce a new style of 'speech-song'—*stile rappresentivo* or *recitative,* ie a melody with a chordal accompaniment—a concept that was a total departure from polyphony.

The harmonic character of the chordal accompaniment brought with it awareness and appreciation of several tones heard simultaneously as a block of sound as opposed to the moving streams of individual melodies approaching, meeting and departing from each other point counter point. When the chordal accompaniment of the recitative acquired tonal centers, and points of repose were felt, music began to shift from modality towards tonality. Medieval folk singers had accompanied themselves with plucked strings, but it was during the baroque era that the system of chordal progression that continues as a dominant force in the music of today was established. Two modes, major and minor, replaced the multiple ecclesiastical modes of former times, accomplishing the transition from mode to key which had begun to be felt in the late Renaissance.

Johann Sebastian Bach superbly realized in his music the fusion of the old and new styles, but even within his lifetime his music, the crowning glory of the Baroque, was considered out-moded. At his death in 1750 it was as though everything that could be said in the 'old style' had been said, so resolute was the turning away from it. Polyphony was to be no longer a way of musical life.

The harpsichord, as it had been in the Renaissance, continued to be in the Baroque the prevailing keyboard instrument of secular and non-liturgical music (the organ was then as now the basic keyboard instrument of the church). At first merely sharing a bass line played by a *viola da gamba,* cello or other low-voiced instrument, it supplied harmony that was indicated by figures appearing with the notes. (Indeed, the baroque period is known as the 'age of the figured-bass' or *basso continuo.*)

Throughout the era individual instruments came into their own. No longer satisfied with leaving to the performers the choice of the instruments to play a composition, composers began to specify which ones were to be used and to write with awareness of the peculiar capabilities and limitations of the various families of instruments. Before the end of the Baroque they were writing idiomatically for individual instruments and the harpsichord assumed a more independent role and finally a 'life of its own'.

The vocal style inaugurated by opera was considered by some to be a bizarre innovation. Every trick of expression was tried: *crescendo* and *diminuendo* (not consciously employed earlier to any considerable extent), trills, vibrato, dynamic accents, even gasps and sobs, and other effects which can only be guessed at from texts of the time, in a determination to make the music convey the sense of words and express earthly and human, rather than lofty and abstract, emotions. These vocal practices had their effect on instrumental styles, and techniques of playing instruments underwent a gradual change. Roman orchestras, especially, began to attract attention to their experiments with a new style of dynamic expression and gradation.

The vast body of music of the period includes a glorious literature for solo keyboard instruments. In the Renaissance, organ and harpsichord or even lute and harpsichord had been used interchangeably. Only three or four examples of music printed before 1600 specify stringed keyboard instruments. Earliest among these is a group of pieces published in Venice by Antonio Gardane in 1551 for 'arpichordo, Clavicembalo, Spinette and Manicordi'.

The boastful claim of a work published in 1611 in England is therefore nearly justified: 'Parthenia or the Maydenhead of the first musicke that ever was printed for the Virginalls composed by three famous masters: William Byrd, Dr John Bull and Orlando Gibbons . . .' (The term virginal or virginals was used generically at this date for any member of the plucked-stringed keyboard family.) The pieces in this English collection were written in a manner eminently suitable to the instrument for which they were intended and the seventeenth century witnessed the development and flourishing of a truly harpsichordistic style.

The Elizabethan composers and their followers produced a cherished treasury of harpsichord music before the center of this activity shifted to the continent. There its climax was achieved in the works of Louis and François Couperin, Jean-Phillippe Rameau, Johann Sebastian Bach, George Frideric Handel, Domenico Scarlatti and numerous others. It cannot be charged that the music of these great composers strained the resources of the harpsichord, and yet François Couperin seemed to express a hint of apology for it when in 1713 in the introduction to his first book of harpsichord pieces he wrote: 'The harpsichord is perfect in its compass and brilliant in itself; but as one cannot increase or diminish its sounds, I will be forever grateful to those who by an infinite art supported by taste will succeed in rendering this instrument capable of expression.'

In his *L'art de toucher le clavecin,* published in 1717, Couperin set forth his ideas of performance. These were aimed at achieving greater emotional and sensitive expression and the full realization of the harpsichord's capabilities—an indication that he was advocating improvement in performance rather than changes in the instrument itself.

Nevertheless, the expressive vocal and instrumental style that had been developing for more than 100 years was threatening the harpsichord with obsolescence since *crescendo, diminuendo,* and dynamic accents by means of touch were beyond its scope. A keyboard instrument combining the expressive potential of the clavichord with the sonority of the harpsichord now seemed called for. The moment was ripe for the appearance of the piano. Unknown to Couperin in 1713, it had, in fact, been invented some years earlier in Florence, but it was not to rival seriously the harpsichord for some sixty years.

PLATE 50 (*next page*)
Harpsichord by Burkat Shudi and Johannes Broadwood, London, 1773. Compass CC to f³, 2 × 8', 1 × 4', lute, buff, machine, Venetian swell, six handstops, two pedals (Les Amis du Musée Instrumental du Conservatoire Royal de Musique, Bruxelles). This harpsichord was a gift from King Frederick the Great to Empress Maria Theresa. Joseph Haydn acquired a similar one from Shudi's workshop after the maker's death. Fine as it is, it represents a phase of the decline of the harpsichord and an attempt to compete with the piano, the popularity of which was, by this date a threat. It contains devices to produce effects intended to compensate for the 'limitations' of the instrument, these limitations being in fact the true nature of the harpsichord. One is the 'Venetian swell' invented by Shudi in 1769 and consisting of louvers which can be opened and closed by the pedal on the right to achieve *crescendo and diminuendo.* Another addition is a machine stop for quick changes of registration, operated by the left pedal. In the most idiomatic of music for the harpsichord, however, *crescendo* and *diminuendo* effects are achieved by the addition or subtraction of notes to thicken or thin the musical texture and changes of registration are adequate between sections or at pauses or breaks where

enough time is allowed by the structure of the music.

The Venetian swell is not successful on the harpsichord; open or closed it muffles the sound when it is placed over the soundboard. Nevertheless, it was successfully adopted for organs and was sometimes applied to early pianos including the upright by John Isaac Hawkins in plate 86, and also a square (c. 1790) by Charles Albrecht of Philadelphia, both in the Hugo Worch Collection, Smithsonian Institution.

Another attempt to produce gradation of volume was made as early as 1754 by Jacob Kirckman in England with a device known as 'nag's head swell' in which a hinged portion of the lid is raised and lowered by a pedal. Since it can be operated only when the lid is closed, it, too, is ineffective musically. It is, however, quite comical visually; when the flap of the lid opens and closes the harpsichord suggests some curious monster gasping for air. The idea was used by Erard in the piano shown in plate 63.

50

5

PIANOS

Some experiments with new types of keyboard instruments were made early in the baroque era. Two instruments called *piano e forte* were mentioned in letters to the Duke of Modena in 1598. Provocative though the name is and tempting as it is to imagine them to be early pianos, no description exists. In 1600 Hans Haydn of Nürnberg attempted a mechanism for bowing the strings of a harpsichord for an additional effect; a Dutch instrument of 1610 having hammers attached to keys but without dampers is said to have been known at one time in a Paris collection; Marin Mersenne, in his treatise of 1636, *Harmonie Universelle,* showed a xylophone with keys, the ends of which struck the bars of wood from below.

Fig. 5
Mersenne's keyed
xylophone

In Paris in 1708, Cuisinié experimented along the line of Haydn's earlier attempt to make a more expressive keyboard instrument. A treadle-operated resined wheel was attached to an instrument whose strings were struck by tangents similar to those of a clavichord; both hands of the performer were free to play on the keyboard while the resined wheel bowed the strings much in the manner of a hurdy-gurdy. These and other similar isolated ventures, however, had no perceptible influence on the evolution of the piano.

BARTOLOMEO CRISTOFORI AND THE FLORENTINE PIANO

Sometime before 1700, Bartolomeo Cristofori, a harpsichord-maker in charge of the musical instrument collection of Prince Ferdinand dei Medici in Florence, replaced harpsichord jacks with leather topped hammers activated by a remarkable mechanical system. The result was an instrument capable of being played loud or soft, of making dynamic accents, and of producing gradations of sound. Not quite aware that he had invented a new instrument, the maker called it *gravicembalo col piano e forte*—harpsichord with soft and loud.

Apart from the hammers, the most striking differences between Cristofori's *gravicembalo col piano e forte* and the other struck-stringed keyboard instrument then in use, the clavichord, were the substitution of hammers covered with leather for metal tangents, a wing-shaped rather than a rectangular instrument, a synchronized damper system, and, most important, an action introducing an 'escapement'. The last feature is essential to a completely successful piano.

The mechanism or the 'action' of a piano involves the tossing of a hammer against a string or several strings tuned in unison. Once the hammer has struck it must immediately fall back from the strings so that they may continue vibrating—a process contrived by a system of levers. Dynamic control is aided by an arrangement that causes the final toss of the hammer to take place from a point quite close to the strings just at the instant the key is fully depressed. The hammer then drops back farther than the distance of this final leap in order to be ready to play again. The mechanism that controls the hammer's upward course and its rebound is known as 'escapement'.

Further refinements are a back-check and a synchronized damper system. The back-check cushions the rebound of the hammer to prevent its bouncing up again from the excess energy of the stroke on the key and bobbing against the strings causing a loss of tone.

In the damper system each key has its own damper that sits on the strings until the hammer strikes them and lifts off at that instant, leaving the strings free to vibrate as long as the key is held down. When the key is released the damper returns to its place.

Cristofori's remarkable invention is the basis of the action of present-day pianos. More than 100 years were to elapse before it was significantly improved.

His first back-check is a pair of crossed threads that cradles the hammer as it falls, but his later version is an upright of wood covered with a soft material that provides enough friction to discourage the hammer's undesirable return. This latter device is still in use.

In 1711 an Italian intellectual, Scipione Maffei, published an article reporting that he had seen four of the new pianos.[18] The date 1709 usually given for the invention of the piano seems to have been based on the year of Maffei's visit to the maker's workshop. We know now, however, that the invention was accomplished sometime between 1693 (when Cristofori was summoned by the prince to Florence from his native Padua) and the year 1700.[19]

Cristofori made some changes between his earliest pianos and the im-

Bartolomeo Cristofori

proved model of 1726 (plate 51). The sketch and explanation below were included in Maffei's enthusiastic article.[20]

Fig. 6
Cristofori piano action

A String
B Frame of the keyboard
C The key or first lever, which at its extremity raises the second lever
D The block on the first lever by which it acts
E The second-lever, on each side of which is a jawbone-shaped piece to support the little tongue or hopper
F The pivot of the second lever
G The movable tongue (hopper), which, being raised by the second lever (E), forces the hammer upwards
H The jawbone-shaped pieces between which the hopper is pivoted
I The strong brass wire pressed together at the top, which keeps the hopper in its place
L The spring of brass wire that goes under the hopper and holds it pressed firmly against the wire which is behind it
M The receiver in which all the butts of the hammers rest
N The circular part of the hammers, which rests in the receiver
O The hammer, which, when pressed upwards by the hopper, strikes the string with the leather on its top
P The strings of silk, crossed, on which the stems, or shanks, of the hammers rest
Q The end of the second lever (E), which becomes lowered by the act of striking the key
R The dampers, which are lowered when the key is touched, leaving the string free to vibrate, and stop the sound on returning to their places
S Part of the frame to strengthen the receiver

Cristofori's piano seems to have attracted little general attention in Italy in his lifetime, but a year after his death in 1731 a set of sonatas was written for it and published in Florence. A manuscript is preserved at the British Museum. Dynamic changes are significantly indicated in the score by the terms *forte, piano, piu piano* and in one instance *piu forte*. These compositions are the earliest published music for piano. The title page reads (in translation):

Sonatas
for harpsichord with soft and loud commonly called
with small hammers
dedicated
to His Royal Highness
the Most Serene Prince D. Antonio
of Portugal
and composed
by D. Lodovico Giustini di Pistoia
first work
Florence 1732

The dedication is to the son of the King of Portugal. Both Prince Antonio and his sister Princess Maria Barbara were lovers of music and were devoted pupils of Domenico Scarlatti, who accompanied the princess to the Spanish court when she married the Spanish king in 1729.

Perhaps the prince played the Giustini sonatas on the Florentine pianos, but Scarlatti took little interest in pianos (although there are said to have been five of them in the Spanish court at one time[21]) and continued to compose his incomparable sonatas for harpsichord.

Cristofori's few pupils went their separate ways at his death; at least one may have found his way to Dresden to influence the beginnings of piano-making there. Another, Giovanni Ferrini, made the piano that was used at the Spanish court in Scarlatti's time by the famous *castrato* singer, Farinelli.

GOTTFRIED SILBERMANN AND THE PIANO

It often happens that when the time is ripe several people conceive the same idea at about the same time—so it was with the invention of the piano. It was, to borrow a phrase from Victor Hugo, 'an idea whose time had come'.

One stimulus was the remarkable playing of an oversized dulcimer by one Pantaleon Hebenstreit. Hebenstreit's gargantuan hammered dulcimer was more than 9ft long—twice the size of those in general use—and had two soundboards, one strung with over-spun catgut, the other with wire strings, some 185 in all.

He played it with stunning virtuosity using double-faced hammers, one side of hard, the other of soft leather. His performances were admired as early as 1697, and when he played for Louis XIV he was honored by the king's proposal that his instrument be called the 'pantaleon'. It allowed for great contrast in dynamics and variety of tone color, but its popularity with other performers was limited due to the extreme difficulty of playing and maintaining it.

Hebenstreit's appearance in Paris in 1705 possibly gave Jean Marius the ideas for four models of *'clavecins à maillets'*—harpsichords with mallets—two of which had down-striking actions: mechanized pantaleons, as it were. These were crude in comparison to the Cristofori instruments and they had no dampers or provision for escapement. Marius showed them at the Royal Academy of Sciences of Paris in 1716, but if the ideas were ever transformed into instruments, which is doubtful, they were quickly forgotten.

In 1714 Hebenstreit became pantaleonist in the court orchestra at Dresden, and in 1717 Christoph Gottlieb Schröter, an organist, writer and instrument maker, after hearing him there, devised two piano actions, one up-striking and one down-striking. Yet in spite of his claim to have invented the piano in Germany, there is no evidence that he succeeded in incorporating his ideas in a musical instrument.

Gottfried Silbermann, a great German organ-builder, was, however, more persistent. He, too, had admired Hebenstreit's playing, and had begun making pantaleons until restrained by an edict prohibiting imitations of the original. Meanwhile, Maffei's article on the Cristofori piano had been translated into German. Probably this translation, along with his experiences with pantaleons, inspired Silbermann to make two pianos which he showed to Johann Sebastian Bach in 1736. Bach admired the tone but complained that the action was heavy and the upper register weak. Silbermann was discouraged, yet his interest did not flag and he continued working on his pianos. After ten more years, during which he very possibly saw a Cristofori instrument, courage again in hand, he brought one of them to the attention of King Frederick II of Prussia (later known as Frederick the Great). The king was delighted and some accounts say he acquired fifteen Silbermann pianos. Only three, however, have survived into this century (plate 53).

The next year Bach went to Potsdam to visit his son, Carl Phillip Emmanuel, chamber-musician to King Frederick since 1740. The older Bach was invited to the palace and led around the various rooms to try the pianos. Whether he was genuinely enthusiastic or merely deferential to royalty is difficult to tell from contemporary accounts, but he was more favorably impressed this time and he obligingly improvised a fugue on a subject supplied by the king. There was little opportunity in the three years left to him to indulge in experimentation with a new instrument, but the event is immortalized in his final great work, *The Musical Offering,* developed from King Frederick's theme. Silbermann is credited, with the inauguration of piano-making in Germany, and for a time it was believed by some in the country that he was the inventor of the piano.

HARPSICHORD TO PIANO

In the 'twilight zone' between rejection of the harpsichord and full acceptance of the piano many experiments were tried in an effort to prolong the life of the harpsichord (see plate 50). Conversely, early piano-makers, as though loath to abandon the harpsichord once and for all, added stops which lowered strips of metal, leather, or cloth on to the strings to suggest a harpsichord sound. One of the Silbermann pianos in the palace at Potsdam has a *cembalo* stop, indication of frank nostalgia.

In the last years of the eighteenth century, some makers were producing harpsichords and pianos in the same workshop. One of these was Pascal Taskin, a great French maker (see page 43) (plate 62). A few instruments were made combining the two with one manual for the harpsichord and a second for the piano, or with a set of hammers superimposed on the harpsichord action and put into operation by means of a pedal.

Several composers including C. P. E. Bach and Jacob Kirkman of the harpsichord-making family wrote compositions for two performers—one playing harpsichord and the other the piano—a medium possible only on the early pianos with a light tone that does not overpower the harpsichord. These compositions were scarcely more successful than the combination instruments.

There was, naturally, some resistance to change. No doubt many agreed with Voltaire when in 1774 he called the piano, compared with the harpsichord, 'a boiler-maker's instrument'. But Charles Burney, the English music-historian, having described pianos and improvements in their mechanisms, said that 'the harsh scratching [!] of the quills of a harpsichord can now no longer be borne'.[22]

Some musical families acquired the 'new-fangled' instruments without discarding their cherished harpsichords. An inventory made by the Commission Temporaire des Arts of instruments confiscated during the French Revolution listed sixty-two harpsichords and spinets, 'the rarest in their perfection', designated (though few reached their destination) to be sent to the Conservatory 'to serve as models because of their working principles'. Twenty-five of the houses where these were found also contained pianos.

Well before the end of the eighteenth century, however, the musical world had begun to recognize that the piano was here to stay, and that it was not simply an 'improved' harpsichord or clavichord, but a different instrument that required a new style of composition. Some consider the three sonatas composed in 1773 by Muzio Clementi, the famous pianist and enterprising London publisher and dealer in musical instruments, to be the first music in a style completely suited to piano. These sonatas established the form of the classical piano sonata. Mozart and Haydn were quick to meet the challenge and others followed suit.

Meanwhile, economic and social factors influenced the increased use of the piano. Clavichords were inexpensive but their uses were limited. Harpsichords cost more than the early pianos and, requiring frequent requilling, were more difficult to maintain. The material resources of the rising middle class encouraged musical amateurs and created a climate favorable to the new keyboard instrument.

Mozart's mother had written to her husband from Mannheim in 1777: 'Everyone thinks the world of Wolfgang here, but indeed he plays quite differently from what he used to in Salzburg [plate 46]—for there are pianofortes here, on which he plays so extraordinarily well that people say they have never heard the like.'[23] Mozart's own important keyboard compositions, except for the early concerto arrangements of works by other composers, are for piano and were written in true pianistic style like those of Haydn. After 1777 Mozart turned more and more to the piano. In plate 60, a painting of 1781 preserved in the Mozart residence in Salzburg, he is seen playing piano duets with his sister—doubtless one of the four-hand compositions for piano that he wrote in the 1780s.

ENGLAND

There is a tradition that an English monk in Rome built a piano and sold it to Samuel Crisp, a friend of Dr. Johnson. Presumably he knew the Cristofori pianos. In England it attracted attention only as a curiosity but a London harpsichord maker, Roger Plenius, copied it and made an unsuccessful attempt to found a piano business. England was not yet ready to abandon the harpsichord.

While experimentation, invention and rivalry were lively among piano makers in Germany, once a workable instrument had been developed, it was not until 1760 that piano making was seriously undertaken in England. In that year twelve piano craftsmen, some of them from Gottfried Silbermann's workshop, came to England to escape the turmoil of the Seven Years' War.

Johannes Zumpe and the eleven other makers coming from Germany in 1760 brought with them traditions owed to both Silbermann and Cristofori. Zumpe, who had been a pupil of Silbermann, had the good fortune to be taken into Burkat Shudi's harpsichord workshop (Plates 41, 42) as did a young man, John Broadwood, coming from Scotland the following year (Plate 50). The history of piano-making owes much to these men.

Zumpe developed a piano action which was a simplification of the Cristofori-Silbermann ideas and, returning to the clavichord shape, installed it in an oblong horizontal case. This instrument unaccountably came to be known as a 'square' piano (plate 55).

The arrival of Johann Christian Bach in London in 1762 was auspicious for both Zumpe and the future of the piano. This youngest son of Johann Sebastian came to prefer the piano over the harpsichord and in 1768 gave the first solo piano performance in an English concert using a Zumpe square.

For reasons unknown—perhaps as an economy measure—Zumpe omitted in his pianos the escapement and the check so cleverly worked out by his predecessors. Despite this obvious disadvantage, his little compact economical pianos soon acquired a great vogue not only in England but on the continent as well. They could scarcely be made fast enough to supply the demand and their maker prospered. Before long, square pianos became so widespread that it is said they were found even in the harems of Middle Eastern countries, where they were supposed to be equipped with short legs so that the performer could be seated on cushions on the floor. In a painting of an English family in their Florentine villa between 1772 and 1776, it is not surprising, therefore, to see them making music with what is, almost certainly, a Zumpe piano[25] brought with them from home (plate 56).

The Zumpe mechanism came to be known as the 'English single action'. Later John Geib, a German working for Longman and Broderip in London, added an escapement and patented his 'English double action' in 1786 which was used in more expensive square pianos. The so-called English action is, in fact, international in its development. Invented in Italy by Cristofori, carried on in Germany by Silbermann, adapted to English needs by Zumpe, a German, it was refined and developed by another German, John Geib. It eventually emerged as the successful English grand action first made by John Broadwood, a Scot, who gave much of the credit for its success to Robert Stodart, an Englishman, and Americus Backers from Holland.

GERMANY AND VIENNA

While Gottfried Silbermann was making pianos with mechanisms derived from the Cristofori pianos, some German instrument makers began making pianos with a different mechanisms. It is not known when the first successful pianos of this latter type were made but there are examples dating from the 1740's.

Gottfried Gottlieb Schröter's claim to having invented the piano had some supporters but, aside from Silbermann, the first name to be considered seriously in connection with the German piano is Johann Andreas Stein.

In October of 1777 Mozart, in a letter to his father from Augsburg, mentioned the pianos of Johann Stein:

This time I shall begin at once with Stein's pianos. Before I had seen any of his make, Späth's claviers had always been my favourites.[26] But now I much prefer Stein's for they damp ever so much better than the Regensburg instruments. When I strike hard, I can keep my finger on the note or raise it, but the sound ceases the moment I have produced it. In whatever way I touch the keys, the tone is always even. It never jars, it is never stronger or weaker or entirely absent; in a word it is always even . . . His instruments have this special advantage over others that they are made with escape action. Only one maker in a hundred bothers about this. But without an escapement it is impossible to avoid jangling and vibration after the note is struck. When you touch the keys, the hammers fall back again the moment after they have struck the strings, whether you hold down the keys or release them[27] [plate 57].

Stein had learned organ-building in Strasbourg from Johann Andreas Silbermann, a nephew of the famous Gottfried. When he began piano-making sometime after settling in Augsburg in 1750, he experimented not with the Gottfried Silbermann type of pianos but with the kind of action developed quite independently by a group of Bavarian makers who were apparently aiming at an improved clavichord. Their first efforts were crude (plate 54), but the idea eventually produced a fine piano accepted by Mozart, Haydn, Beethoven and others. These craftsmen—no single name stands out among them—had developed a *Prellemechanik*, which Stein improved by adding an escapement.

It is not clear when Joseph Haydn made his first acquaintance with the piano or even when pianos were first acquired at Esterháza. Anton Walter had an appointment at the palace in 1781 that may have lead to the acquisition of one or the regulation and tuning of one already there. Since Haydn in 1788 asked his publisher, Artaria, to pay for a *new* piano he had ordered from Johann Wenzel Schantz, it could not have been his first. Certainly he had abandoned the harpsichord well before 1790, for in a letter in February of that year, melancholy about returning from Vienna to Esterháza, he wrote to his cherished friend Marianne von Genzinger: 'Nothing could console me; my whole lodging was in disorder; my piano that I usually love in other times was moody and disobedient and provoked my displeasure more than it consoled me.'[24] Not a word about his harpsichord. (Among his instruments at the time were a Shudi and Broadwood harpsichord mentioned earlier, his Schantz piano and a clavichord. Only the last instrument has survived and he used it for composing until the end of his life.) He urged Madame von Genzinger to buy a piano saying he could no longer compose for a harpsichord.

For a century and a half Viennese and English actions both enjoyed favor. (The term 'fortepiano' is frequently used today for any eighteenth-century German piano. The English piano of the time, however, was usually called 'pianoforte.') Some preferred the light touch and tone of the former, others the more resistant touch and powerful tone of the latter. Many makers produced both types in their workshops in order to cater to the inclinations of their clients. The last pianos with Viennese action were made during the opening years of the twentieth century. The modern piano is based on the Cristofori-Silbermann-English principles and certain refinements added to it have produced a piano with a degree of the touch sensitive quality claimed for the Viennese action (plates 58, 59).

Beethoven grew up with the Viennese piano and never abandoned it even after he possessed Erard and Broadwood instruments. When he began his career, the harpsichord was seldom heard except as a support instrument in orchestras and to accompany recitative in opera.

After the daughter of J. A. Stein, Nannette Stein-Streicher, the first and only woman to attain prominence in the piano industry, moved to Vienna she became Beethoven's devoted and protective friend. Both benefited from conversations on piano construction from the points of view of composer-performer and builder.

Although Gottfried Silbermann built the first successful piano in Germany, it was the Stein action that came to be known as 'German' and later 'Viennese.'

Toward the end of the eighteenth century Vienna had many makers of fine pianos such as Anton Walter whose pianos Mozart favored after he settled in Vienna, Wenzel Schantz, favored by Joseph Haydn, and his brother Johann, Matthäus Stein and Nannette Stein-Streicher, the children of J. A. Stein who moved to Vienna after their father's death, and Conrad Graf who by 1815 was considered by many to be the foremost maker of grands. Before these makers, however, the history of the piano is murky due in part to the inability of makers to agree on consistent terminology, using a mixture of terms that could indicate either harpsichords, pianos or even clavichords; the terms fortepiano or pianoforte were not applied consistently until the 1780's. A recently found document proved that a piano was played in concert in Vienna in 1760.

POSSIBILITIES AND PROBLEMS

As the possibilities of the piano were realized, composers and performers made more and more demands of it. Program or descriptive music became the rage of the late eighteenth century. This was no new idea—the biblical sonatas of Johann Kuhnau and the harpsichord pieces of Rameau and Couperin with descriptive titles such as *La Poule (The Hen)* and *Le Rappel des Oiseaux (The Call of the Birds)* were not isolated examples—but a taste indulged by some early nineteenth-century composers to imitate booming canons, thunder, the sound of waves, and other natural phenomena were bound to strain the resources of the piano.

The problem of sustaining a note also became a matter of concern. Clavichord performers had been able to accomplish this with some success by the use of vibrato *(Bebung),* and harpsichord composers had ornamented with trills and turns a note to be prolonged. Pianists continued the practice of ornamentation and also adopted the expedient of fast repetition of a note to carry over its sound. Earlier piano actions could not articulate adequately for these performance devices.

Other problems plagued makers. Greater volume was not only desired by composers and performers for expressing more powerful, dramatic, *fortissimo* writing, but needed, too, for larger concert halls and orchestras. To meet this demand string tension was increased, necessitating heavier stringing and placing greater stress on the frame of the piano. Additional stress was created by the increasing keyboard compass, pushing up to $7\frac{1}{4}$ octaves (AAA to c^5) before the end of the nineteenth century, and by the elevation of pitch. This rose from as low as 415 cycles to the second for a^1 to 421.6 in Mozart's time and as high as 456 later in Vienna before 440 was established by the International Standards Association in 1939.[28] Experiments which continue unceasingly today were constantly being tried to produce a piano with a more resonant and more beautiful tone, an action responsive and dependable under all conditions, and tuning and mechanism that remain stable in atmospheric changes.

These qualities are determined in a number of ways: the degree of communication between the strings and the soundboard accomplished by the strings constantly pressing the bridge firm against the soundboard that is forced up by the framing (ie crowned) into a slightly convex shape; the resonant capacity of the soundboard; the nature of the material of the strings and of the covering of the hammers; the arrangement and the determination of the gauges of the strings; the point at which the hammer strikes the strings; a hammer action capable of reacting to a powerful stroke or to a light delicate touch and of restriking a note with great rapidity; control of extreme changes in the various materials due to fluctuations of temperature and humidity.

Every aspect of the construction of the piano has come under critical scrutiny: the action has constantly been re-studied for means of improvement; for the soundboard many kinds of wood and seasoning have been tried as well as variations in the thickness and in the direction of the grain of the wood; the thin leather covering of the hammers was supplemented by cloth under the leather, and a variety of other materials were tried before the shaped layers of felt used today were adopted; experiments were made in covering the steel strings with copper or silver for greater elasticity, and in the manner of securing them at both ends; and a faster-acting and more responsive damper pedal was developed.

Along with efforts to improve and refine piano action and tone a remarkable assortment of cabinet styles were designed (plates 66, 68, 73, 74, 75, 80) small and large uprights as well. While new styles of piano composition were being created and performance techniques developed, the piano became more important to family and social life (plates 64, 65, 72, 81, 82).

Even before the end of the eighteenth century the piano—no longer the exclusive property of kings and noblemen—began to be found in the homes of the rising middle class. Once Zumpe had shown the practicality and saleability of a piano more economical to make and easier to accommodate in a modest setting, others began to occupy themselves with new sizes and shapes. Early experiments had been made to develop a vertical instrument (plate 66) before William Stodart of London, looking back to the clavicytherium (plate 26) brought out in 1795 his 'upright grand'—a small grand up-ended, installed in a rectangular case and set on a stand (plate 68). This was more successful than previous attempts at a vertical piano and others followed his example.

Pianos were sometimes provided with pedal boards on which the lowest notes could be played (plate 61). Earlier some clavichords, harpsichords and virginals were so equipped. These were intended primarily for organ practice.

Between 1716 and 1851 an astonishing number of patents[20] were registered for ideas dealing with every aspect of the craft. Some never got beyond the drawing board; others were tried and abandoned and still others were refined, developed and adopted as standard. The history of the piano through the nineteenth century is opaque with the multiplicity and complexity of experiments and inventions.

FRANCE

The piano is said to have made its first appearance in Paris in 1759. Two Germans, Johann Schobert (1720–67) and Johann Eckhardt (1735–1809) were the first piano virtuosi heard there. They must have played German pianos brought from home. Eckhardt was taken to Paris by the piano maker, Johann Andreas Stein in 1758 and remained there. Stein, an organ builder, did not make his first piano until a few years later so far as we know. Eckhardt lived late enough to have become familiar with English pianos.

Pianos began to arrive in numbers from England after their first appearance in concert there (1767). One Mademoiselle Lechantre played the piano for the first time in concert in Paris in 1768 at the 'Concert Spirituel'. If it was an English piano, it would have been quite new to her. When a celebrated singer in 1771 stated his preference for a piano over a harpsichord, it was likely an English piano.

As mentioned previously, Cuisinié in 1708 had attempted an experiment to make the harpsichord dynamically expressive and in 1716 Jean Marius had submitted models for four *clavecins à maillets* to the Royal Academy of Science. Neither of these ingenious mechanisms was successful. The harpsichord was well entrenched and French composers were writing great music for it.

There is said to have been a piano made in France in 1770 but the earliest important date in French piano history is 1777, the year in which Sébastien Erard made his first piano.

The French writer, Ernest Closson, while recognizing the outstanding achievements of the Viennese school, states that it remained for the English and French makers to bring about new progress and that the inventor of the modern piano was Erard.

Erard had come from Alsace in 1768 and worked first for a harpsichord maker. His first piano was a square model and contained the English type of action probably patterned after Johannes Zumpe's instruments which were already popular in France (Plate 63).

The enterprising Sébastien opened a workshop in London while his brother carried on the business in Paris, and the acquisition of one of their pianos by the First Consul, Napoleon Bonaparte, brought them deserved attention.

Through the succeeding decades the Erards made many contributions to the improvement of the piano, the most important of which is the repetition action developed by Sébastien and patented by his nephew in 1821. Sébastien was familiar with both the English grand action and the Viennese action and achieved a combination of the best qualities of each: the stability and solidity of the former and the sensitive responsiveness of the latter. The repetition or double escapement mechanism is a complicated system of springs and levers which arrest the hammer in its rebound after it has struck the strings. The practical result is that as long as the key is held down the hammer remains close to the strings instead of returning to its original position so that if a note is to be repeated the hammer has a much shorter distance to travel in order to strike the strings again. Its advantage to the performer is obvious: a succession of repeated notes can be executed with greater ease and speed, and dynamic shadings can be more delicately controlled.

The action involved such an intricate assemblage of moving parts that the first examples of it easily went out of order. Moreover the mechanism was noisy. But Erard continued to work on it and Henri Herz, a pianist and inventor, simplified and refined it. The Herz-Erard action met with the full approval of performers and modern action incorporates its principles.

Two other improvements by the Erards were widely adopted: the agraffe—a metal stud pierced with a hole for each string to pass through—invented in 1806 by Sébastien and the harmonic bar, devised by Pierre in 1838. Both of these are for the dual purpose of precisely fixing the down-bearing of the bridge to ensure communication between the bridge and soundboard and to prevent the hammers from dislodging the strings from their proper place on the bridge.

Sébastien Erard is also responsible for a revolutionary improvement in the harp—an arrangement of pedals known as double action making it possible to play in all keys, and which is applied to modern harps.

PIANISTS AND PIANOS

The nineteenth century saw the development of virtuoso piano technique, and piano-makers were hard pressed to meet the demands of pianists like Franz Liszt and Frédéric Chopin.

Liszt with his dazzling heroic style (plates 76, 77) seems to have played any and all pianos in his vigorous concert career; Chopin's expressive style, distinguished by extraordinary delicacy and subtlety of nuance, seems to have been best accommodated by the French pianos of Pleyel (plate 78) and Erard. Liszt said, 'Chopin was fond of Pleyel pianos because of their silvery and somewhat veiled sonority and their easy touch',[30] and Chopin said, 'When I am in a bad mood, I play Erard pianos and easily find in them a ready-made sound. But when I am in good spirits and strong enough to find the sounds I want I use Pleyel pianos.'[31] In 1848 he wrote from London that he had three pianos in his rooms, an Erard, a Pleyel and a Broadwood. In England he customarily played a Broadwood in concert.

John Field and Chopin share credit for the inauguration of a virtuoso pedal technique that increases sustaining power, enhances singing tone, and can even, in a mysterious way, produce a silhouette of a note or line against a background of diffused harmonies, a technique carried to its ultimate in the evanescent magical effects of the impressionistic music of Claude Debussy and Maurice Ravel.

A well-known painting of Franz Liszt surrounded by adoring listeners (plate 76) gives an excellent impression of his romantic aura. More than any other single performer, he raised the status of the performing musician from that of servant to the rich, to one of respect, adulation and glamour. His pianistic virtuosity greatly influenced piano-making. Using the full weight and strength of shoulders, arms and wrists he made the instrument speak with a power, drama, and even violence that it had never done before. His style of playing, as well as his compositions, represent the essence of the Romantic movement. Pianos suffered at his hands and it was not at all unusual for one or more strings to break and for the piano to require retuning in the midst of one of his concerts. In fact, on occasions a spare piano stood ready on the stage and reports of his concerts suggest that the audience felt cheated if a piano survived intact (plate 77). He played the finest available European pianos and on at least one occasion an American Chickering. In his Weimar studio Liszt had a Steinway concert grand.

Piano-playing by women in the nineteenth century was considered an attractive social accomplishment (plate 81) much as playing the virginal was two centuries earlier (plate 31). Some women were serious and highly accomplished pianists, but few followed the example of Clara Schumann (plate 79), daughter of a fine pianist and teacher, wife of Robert Schumann, confidante of Johannes Brahms and the first to play many of his works. Her professional concert career gave courage and inspiration to others of her sex.

Another composer who influenced the development of the piano in the nineteenth century was Beethoven, who often wanted it to sound like an orchestra. In 1818 he received a grand piano as a gift from the Broadwood firm (plate 71), his first six-octave instrument; his last three monumental sonatas were composed after he became its proud owner. His keyboard compositions until the third concerto, published in 1804, were contained within a five-octave compass as were all of Mozart's and most of Haydn's. Erard had presented him with a piano of five and a half octaves (FF to c^4) in 1803 (plate 70).

Beethoven's experiences with pianos were not always happy. The following account by a professor at the Paris Conservatory of a performance by Beethoven that probably took place some time between 1803 and 1808 is vivid evidence that the piano provided at the time was not, to put it mildly, equal to the occasion:

> One evening when Beethoven was playing a Mozart piano concerto . . . he asked me to turn the pages for him. But I was mostly occupied in wrenching out the strings of the piano which snapped, while the hammers stuck among the broken strings. Beethoven insisted upon finishing the concerto, so back and forth I leaped jerking out a string, disentangling a hammer, turning a page, and I worked harder than Beethoven.[32]

Difficulties of a similar nature were plaguing other pianists. Carl Maria von Weber in an unfinished novel describes a scene (perhaps autobiographical) in which the overwrought hero strikes a low C on the piano: 'The hammer flew out of its fork and a number of strings gave up their lives crunchingly—thus did the anger that so violently overwhelmed me dash my hand upon the keys. . . . '[33]

Beethoven wrote to thank the Broadwoods effusively for their gift even before their piano arrived, but once he tried it it can only have been the feel of the heavier action and the extended keyboard compass that gave him pleasure rather than the sound, for in 1818 his deafness, as early as 1798 a matter of extreme anxiety, had progressed to the point that he probably could not judge the quality of the tone. Desperately frustrated, he appealed often to his friends, the Streichers, to adjust his Broadwood or provide another piano audible to him, and he did not wholly abandon the Viennese instruments. In the last years of his life the well-known Viennese maker, Conrad Graf, put at his disposal one of his quadruple-strung pianos in the vain hope that it would be audible to him. It had four strings to a note except for the lowest bass notes and was an attempt to

PLATE 51 *(above)*

Piano by Bartolomeo Cristofori, Florence, Italy, 1726; compass C to c³ (Musikinstrumenten Museum, Karl Marx Universität, Leipzig, Germany). This piano represents the climax of Cristofori's work. It is double-strung, has a synchronized damper system and an *una corda* device, ie a lever underneath the keyboard by means of which one may shift the action so that the hammer strikes only one of a pair of strings for a dynamic contrast.

Like harpsichords of the time it is lightly framed and provided with a heavier ornamented case from which it was removed to be played as it is shown here. Its dimensions are virtually the same as those of a harpsichord by the same maker. An examination reveals that Cristofori was indeed a genius, an imaginative craftsman far in advance of his time.

Two other pianos by him survive: one in the Metropolitan Museum of Art, New York, the other in the Museo Degli Strumenti Musicali, Rome.

PLATE 52 *(left)*

Action of Cristofori's piano of 1726 (Karl Marx Universität, Leipzig). The hammer head is a small block of wood curved on top to hold a hollow cylinder made of layers of thick paper topped with a leather pad for lightness and elasticity.

PLATE 53 *(left)*

Grand piano by Gottfried Silbermann, Freiberg, Germany, c. 1745; compass FF to d³ (Staatliche Schlösser und Garten Potsdam-Sanssouci, Germany). This is one of three Silbermann pianos belonging to Frederick the Great that survived into this century. Two remain in his Sanssouci palace where this one was photographed. The third disappeared but is thought still to be in existence. Silbermann adopted Cristofori's ideas without significant alteration.

PLATE 54 *(left)*

Square piano by Gottlob Emanuel Rüfner, Nürnberg, Germany, c. 1780; compass FF to g³, two hand stops: one raises dampers, the other is a buff stop moving leather tabs between the hammers and strings (Smithsonian Institution, 332,175, Hugo Worch Collection). The crudely made and painted case of this piano, the keyboard surround covered with stamped paper, is indistinguishable in outward appearance from that of one of the simple clavichords of the time; but instead of a clavichord mechanism it houses a primitive piano action—the *Prellemechanik* or bouncing action.

The hammers are upright wedge-shaped pieces of uncovered wood suggestive of the upright clavichord tangents, but the crucial difference is, of course, that the hammer pivoted to a *kapsel* fixed to the key is propelled up to strike the strings and then permitted to rebound instead of pressing against the strings as long as the key is held down as do the clavichord's tangents. There is no escapement or check.

The maker's name is signed by hand on the label attached to the case behind the keys and he further identifies himself as 'organ and instrument maker of Nürnberg'.

The earliest known surviving square piano with the *Prellemechanik* was made in 1742 by Johann Söcher in Upper Bavaria. It is now in the Germanisches Nationalmuseum, Nürnberg. The sophistication of its craftsmanship suggests that it must have had predecessors. Rüfner was doubtless one of many makers of his time trying his hand at the new instrument. It would be interesting to know if the builders of the earliest of these primitive pianos were, like Cristofori, unconscious of having made a new instrument and, like him, thought of their innovation as an improvement of a familiar one.

PLATE 55

Square piano by Johannes Zumpe and Gabriel Buntebart, London, 1770; compass FF to f³ (no FF♯) three hand stops: one presses a felt strip against strings in front of hitch-pins for muted effect, a second raises bass dampers and a third raises treble dampers (Smithsonian Institution, 60,1390, formerly Cooper Union Collection, New York). The piano shown here was made during Zumpe's partnership with Gabriel Buntebart (1769–78) and is typical of his instruments. Throughout his career he disdained the more impressive grand model.

The earliest surviving English piano is the one he made in 1766 that has seventeen notes to the octave for most of its compass producing the shade of difference (nearly a quarter-tone) between the sharps and their nearest flats (ie D♯, E♭, F♯, G♭, etc). It recalls the experiments with enharmonic keyboards made in Italy in the seventeenth century and the virginal by Boni shown in plate 36.[34]

Equal temperament had not yet supplanted mean-tone tuning in England, and Zumpe was influenced to make his experimental keyboard by the writings of Dr Robert Smith of Cambridge who advocated twenty-four notes to the octave for purer tuning in all keys.

Earlier Johann Sebastian Bach had demonstrated the advantages of a tuning system workable in all keys in his forty-eight Preludes and Fugues for Well-Tempered Clavier and ultimately the general acceptance of equal temperament obviated any need for enharmonic keyboards, and mean-tone tuning was largely forgotten.[35]

PLATE 56
The Cowper and Gore Families, painting by John Zoffany (1734–1810) (property of the Honourable Lady Salmond, Hanfield, Sussex, England). This painting of George, 3rd Earl Cowper with his wife, the former Anne Gore, her father and other members of the family, was painted between 1772 and 1776 at the Earl's Florentine villa. Mr Gore is playing the cello held between the knees in the manner of a viola da gamba. It is most likely a piano by Zumpe that is used.[25]

PLATE 57
Grand piano by Johann Andreas Stein, Augsburg; compass FF to f^3, double strung, German action, two knee-levers for raising the dampers (Germanisches Nationalmuseum, Nürnberg, Neupert Collection). The maker is the one whose instruments were much admired by Mozart. This grand piano dates from the 1770s.

PLATE 58
Model of English grand action (Division of Musical Instruments, Smithsonian Institution).

The key A—A is a lever one end of which is struck by the finger. It is held in place by a pin (B) on a fulcrum (K). The hammer (C) is set on the rear end of a shank the front end of which is attached to a small block of wood (O) pivoted to a rail (D) that is part of the frame of the action.

Motion is transmitted to the hammer through the escapement (F), an upright attached to the key. The block of wood at the front of the hammer shank has a notch cut in it that rests on the top of this upright.

When the key is struck the escapement slides back under pressure from the regulating screw (G); when it finally slips out of the notch the hammer that had been travelling up makes its final toss to strike the strings (I). The control of the hammer's upward course until the last instant that is accomplished by the escapement mechanism gives the performer better control over the dynamics than would be possible if the hammer travelled freely from its rest. Once the hammer has struck it drops back against the back-check (E) and remains there as long as the key is held down.

Upon release of the key the back-check moves back allowing the hammer to drop down to its rest (N) and the escapement slips back under the notch in the block of wood as the rear end of the key descends.

The damper system consists of a jack (M) dropped through a mortise in the damper rail, its top capped with a pad of leather and felt (H). The jack is pushed up by the rear end of the key to lift the pad from the strings just as the hammer strikes them. It falls back of its own weight when the key is released.

A Keys
B Pins
C Hammers—the upper one arrested just before the final toss; the other at rest
D Hammer rail (also called hammer beam)
E Back-check
F Escapement (also called hopper or jack)
G Set-off screw to regulate escapement
H Damper
I Strings
J Wrest pins
K Fulcrum
L Hammer shanks
M Damper jack
N Hammer rest
O Notched block of wood (also called butt)

A Keys
B Pins
C Kapsel (hammer sup-
   port or housing)
D Hammers—the upper
   one arrested just before
   the final toss; the other
   at rest
E Back-check
F Escapement
G Spring
H Damper-jack
I Strings
J Wrest pins
K Fulcrum
L Hammer shanks
M Upright that raises
   damper jack
N Hammer rest

Model of German or Viennese action (Division of Musical Instruments, Smithsonian Institution).

The key (A—A) is a lever one end of which is struck by the finger. It is held in place by a pin (B) on a fulcrum (K). The hammer (D) is on the front end of a shank (L) that is pinned at the other end to a Kapsel (C) fixed to the rear of the key. The shank terminates in a beak-shaped projection. The 'beak' rests in a notch in the escapement (F) which is pressed forward at all times by a light spring (G). When the key is struck the Kapsel rises carrying the hammer up and as the beak slips out of the notch in the escapement the hammer is freed to make its final toss to strike the strings (I). The control of the hammer's upward course until the last instant that is accomplished by the escapement mechanism gives the performer better control over the dynamics than would be possible if the hammer travelled freely from its resting place (N) to the strings.

Once the hammer has struck it falls back against the back-check (E) which is covered with material that provides a bit of friction to prevent the hammer from bouncing back to bob undesirably against the strings muffling the tone. It rests there and the beak rests against the escapement above the notch as long as the key is held down. Upon release of the key the hammer drops to its rest (N) as the escapement is pushed back into place by the string (G).

The damper action consists of two parts: a short base of wood (M) cushioned with felt sits on the key and raises as the key is struck pushing up a damper jack (H) to which is attached a thick pad of felt. The felt lifts from the strings the instant the hammer strikes. When the key is released the jack falls down of its own weight, the felt pad coming to rest again on the strings.

PLATE 60

Mozart and his family. Engraving after a painting by Johann Nepomuk de la Croce, 1781 in Mozart's residence, Salzburg (Internationale Stiftung Mozarteum, Salzburg, Austria). Mozart is seen here at the age of twenty-five playing piano duets with his sister, their father an onlooker and their mother's portrait on the wall. The five-octave compass of the keyboard of the time was scarcely wide enough to accommodate two adults. Mozart had composed his first piece for four hands at one keyboard in 1765 at the age of nine when he and his little sister could quite comfortably fit together at a five-octave harpsichord. One wonders how they managed, comfortably, to play the four-hand compositions he wrote in the 1780s.

Charles Burney, the English music-historian (1726–1814) mentioned this eighteenth-century problem in Rees' *Cyclopaedia* for which he contributed articles on music. 'The ladies at that time wearing hoops which kept them too great a distance from one another had a harpsichord by Merlin[36] expressly for duets with six octaves.' Burney's own duets 'for two Performers upon one Piano Forte or Harpsichord' appear to be the first work for keyboard duet to appear in print and he had one of Merlin''s six-octave pianos on which to perform them.[37]

The earliest known composition for two performers at one keyboard is Nicholas Carleton's 'A Verse for Two to Play on one Virginall or Organe' preserved in manuscript in the British Museum and thought to date from the mid-sixteenth century. It has been published in a modern edition.

PLATE 61 (*above left*)

Pedal grand piano. Austria, late eighteenth century, probably by Johann Schmidt; compass FF to a³, pedalboard, EE/CC to A (bass short octave) (Germanisches Nationalmuseum, Rück Collection, Nürnberg, Germany). Pianos were sometimes equipped with pedalboards as were, earlier, some clavichords, harpsichords and virginals. Pedal pianos, harpsichords and clavichords were intended primarily for organ practice, but Robert Schumann wrote a few compositions especially for pedal piano including six lovely pieces in canon (1845) now heard in transcription for two pianos.

Johann Schmidt was recommended by Mozart's father to the Salzburg court as an organ-builder, and Mozart, therefore, was probably familiar with his instruments.

PLATE 62 (*above right*)

Grand piano by Pascal Taskin, Paris, 1788; compass FF to f³, two knee-levers for raising dampers (Musée Instrumental du Conservatoire National Supérieur de Musique, Paris). Among harpsichord-makers keeping up with the times by making pianos along with harpsichords was Pascal Taskin. This is the earliest of the three grands known to have been made by him. Another dated 1789 is in the Musikinstrumenten-Museum, Staatliches Institut für Musikforschung, Berlin, and the third is in the Petit Trianon, Versailles. The beautiful instrument shown here is indistinguishable, by its outward appearance, from a harpsichord. Its case and the soundboard ornamented with painted flowers are in typical French harpsichord style.

75

PLATE 64
Mantle clock. Bronze work by Antoine André Ravrio, Paris, 1805–10 (Cooper-Hewitt Museum of Decorative Arts and Design, Smithsonian Institution, New York). The choice of a piano as a decorative motive in this handsome empire-style clock-case suggests the important place the piano had assumed in French society by the early nineteenth century.

PLATE 63 (*facing page, above*)

Square piano by Erard Frères et Cie, Paris, 1799; compass FF to c⁴, three knee-levers, one knee-lever raises a flap of the lid for a swell effect, a second raises dampers and the third is a buff stop raising a thin strip of soft leather against the strings (Smithsonian Institution, 315,677, Hugo Worch Collection). The Erard piano illustrated here is equipped with the curious device known as 'nag's head swell' earlier applied to some harpsichords by Jacob Kirckman (see p 50). Impractical when used as intended, it was operated in a novel if unmaidenly way by a certain young lady who, it is reported,[38] owned a pianoforte with two pedals, one for sustaining the sound and the other for opening the short side of the lid for the purpose of obtaining a 'swell' effect. When she played battle pieces she illustrated exploding cannon by suddenly releasing her knee from the swell lever, permitting the lid to fall with a realistic bang.

PLATE 65

Family of Lucien de Bonaparte, 1815. Drawing by Jean Auguste Dominique Ingres, France, 1786–1867 (Fogg Art Museum, Harvard University, Cambridge, Mass). Here two ladies of the family play lyre guitar and a piano—French instruments evidently taken to Rome by the family upon Lucien's retirement to that city. The drawing was done in Rome.

PLATE 66 (*above left*)

Pyramidal piano by Christian Ernst Friederici, Germany, 1745 (Les Amis du Musée Instrumental du Conservatoire de Musique, Bruxelles). Early experiments in developing a vertical piano were made by Friederici who tried two versions of a pyramidal instrument. In one attributed to him he grouped the long bass strings in the middle and arranged the treble strings on each side, necessitating an action with a kind of tracker system, a mechanism familiar to Friederici from his organ-building. In the later model, shown here and in the following plate, he arranged the strings diagonally over the soundboard. The result was a handsome, but fanciful, instrument.

PLATE 67 (*above right*)

Interior view of the pyramidal piano of the preceding plate.

PLATE 68
Upright grand piano by John Broadwood and Sons, London, c. 1815;
compass CC to c⁴, two pedals: *una corda,* and split pedal to raise treble and
bass dampers separately if desired (Smithsonian Institution, 303,529,
Hugo Worch Collection).

Looking back perhaps to the clavicytherium (plate 26), William
Stodart of London brought out in 1795 his 'upright grand': a simple idea
in which a small grand is up-ended, installed in a rectangular case and set
on a stand. This was more successful than Friederici's earlier idea for a
vertical piano (plates 66, 67) and carrying practicality still further,
Stodart thoughtfully utilized the space left by the bent side by adding
shelves for storing books or music.

PLATE 69
Interior view of the Broadwood piano shown in the
preceding plate.

The Broadwood piano shown here uses Stodart's plan. The action
strikes from back to front through an opening in the soundboard, a plan
equivalent to the up-striking action usual for a horizontal instrument.
Down-striking action was tried from time to time in horizontal instruments, but was abandoned due to the difficulty of achieving a prompt
rebound. Before the end of the nineteenth century, however, a front-to-
back action became standard in principle for uprights.

The split damper pedal for controlling treble and bass dampers separately suggests interesting possibilities for use when one hand is called
upon to play *staccato* and the other *legato*. Beethoven's piano of 1817 (plate
71) and the early grand of 1811 in plate 72 have such an arrangement. It
was ultimately discarded.

As with the upright harpsichord or clavicytherium, the action of the vertical piano must have a spring mechanism to aid the hammers and dampers to fall back into place, since this is not accomplished by the force of gravity as is the case in the horizontal instruments.

This piano stands nearly 9ft tall and is threateningly top heavy.

PLATE 70

Grand piano by Sébastien Erard, Paris, 1801; compass FF to c⁴, four pedals, one *una corda* knee-lever (Finchcocks Collection, Richard Burnett, Goudhurst, Kent). The four pedals are: bassoon on lower strings; damper; moderator (which moves forward felt tabs through which the hammers then strike; each tab is graduated in thickness and an extremely subtle gradation of dynamics can be achieved by slowly depressing and releasing the pedal); *due corda*. (The bassoon pedal is explained on p95.)

Except for the knee-lever this is like the piano the Erard firm presented to Beethoven in 1803. He was never fond of it and it can be conjectured that one reason was the complicated pedal system. Although extraordinary coloristic effects can be achieved with the four pedals, they are tricky to use.

PLATE 71 *(above left)*
Grand piano by John Broadwood and Sons, London, 1817; compass CC to
c⁴, two pedals: *una corda* and split pedal for controlling treble and bass
dampers separately (National Museum, Budapest, Hungary). This piano
was the one given to Beethoven by the Broadwoods.

PLATE 72 *(above right)*
Piano by Broadwood and Sons, London, 1811; and *The Sisters*. Painting by
Sir William Beechey, England, c. 1830 (Huntington Galleries, George L.
Bagby Collection, Huntington, West Virginia). The piano in the fore-
ground of this photograph is a near twin in all important respects to the
one illustrated in the preceding plate. It was obviously a proud possession,
as seen in the painting above it.

PLATE 73 (*above left*)
Giraffe piano by Martin Seuffert, Vienna, c. 1812; compass FF to f⁴, two pedals: *una corda* and damper (Smithsonian Institution, 315,657, Hugo Worch Collection). In the piano presented here the case adheres to the shape of the up-ended grand, unlike the Broadwood in plates 68 and 69. A good number of these so-called giraffe pianos were made, many with quite handsomely decorated cases, their elegance belying the incongruous appellation that was applied to them.

PLATE 73a (*above right*)
The Tender Chord, painting by Sir William Orchardson. England, c. 1886 (Collection unknown). Shows giraffe piano by Van der Hoef of Amsterdam.

PLATE 74

Upright piano by Wilkinson and Wornum, London, c. 1812; compass FF to c⁴, two pedals: one slides pads of felt against strings for a muted effect, a second raises dampers (Smithsonian Institution, 315,673, Hugo Worch Collection). Many designs for small pianos were tried. A model patented by the English maker, William Collard, in 1798, was simply a square piano turned up on its side and placed on a stand. William Southwell's 'piano sloping backward' was a similar arrangement, but with the piano tipped back from the performer; the designer claimed that his model was more comfortable for the performer and obligingly equipped it with a device for turning pages by means of a pedal.

The piano shown here is an early example of the small pianos introduced by Robert Wornum. The back is covered with the same wood and finished in the same way as the front and sides so that the instrument may be seen from any angle and need not be placed against the wall as with the usual uprights. Since this piano is only 41in tall the performer's head could be seen above it, a particular advantage to the self-accompanied singer.

In 1813 Wornum brought out a small upright with vertical stringing reaching to the floor and utilizing all the available space, a type which he called a 'Cottage' piano. In 1838 he listed a variety of other models: the 'Piccolo' which stood 3ft 8in, the 'Cabinet' (ie tall upright), the 'Pocket Grand Horizontal', only 5ft 4in long, and the 'Imperial Grand Horizontal'.[39] The small pianos were copied by European makers, including Pleyel in France who called them 'Pianinos'.

PLATE 75

Table piano made by Jean-Henri Pape, Paris, mid-nineteenth century; compass FF to f⁴, two pedals; formerly the property of the Duke of Wellington (Gallini Collection, Civico Museo Degli Strumenti Musicali, Castello Sforzesco, Milano, Italy). For a time there was a vogue for dual-purpose pianos—miniature boudoir- or sewing-tables, or writing-desks, the tops of which opened to reveal the piano keys of their secret musical lives.

Jean-Henri Pape can be forgiven the ungainly piece of furniture housing this piano if one recalls that he patented many ideas aimed at improving piano action, and that he made, in 1826, a very significant contribution by his development of a satisfactory felt for covering the hammers—the first time felt replaced deer skin for this purpose. In 1839 he designed a hammer-cover of tapered layers of treated felt—the type still in use. German makers were the last to give up the deer skin covering and resisted the use of felt until the early 1850s. The hammers of a modern grand piano developed from Pape's ideas are shown in plate 98.

85

PLATE 76

Liszt at the Piano. Painting by Joseph Danhauser, Vienna, 1840 (National Galerie der Stiftung Preussischer Kulturbesitz, Berlin). This purports to be a painting of Liszt with Alexandre Dumas and Georges Sand, seated, Victor Hugo, Paganini and Rossini, standing, and the Countess d'Agoult swooning in ecstasy, her head against the piano. A bust of Beethoven, also by Danhauser, dominates the scene. A photograph of Lord Byron hangs on the wall.

The instrument shows the mark of Conrad Graf, well-known Viennese maker. This realistic touch notwithstanding, the presence of Victor Hugo arouses a suspicion that the painting does not record an actual event. Hugo did not like music and when some of his poems were set to music asked disdainfully, 'Why, aren't they musical enough?'[40]

PLATE 77
Liszt et Son Sabre. From *La Vie Parisienne,* 3 April 1886 (Library of Congress, Washington, DC). Liszt fully exploited the tonal resources of the piano both in his compositions and performances. His extravagant flamboyant style and his assaults upon the keyboard are caricatured here with the translated caption:

> LISZT AND HIS SWORD—that he has renounced today, after having recognised that he was doing more harm to the piano with his hands alone. Strange specimen of the race of creatures with tentacles. Eight hands with four octaves each, thirty-two octaves!!![41]

LISZT ET SON SABRE. — Y a renoucé aujourd'hui, après avoir reconnu qu'il faisait plus de mal au piano avec ses seules mains. Spécimen étrange de la race des tentaculifères. Huit mains à quatre octaves chacune, trente-deux octaves!!!.

PLATE 78
Grand piano by Ignace Pleyel et Cie, France; compass CC to g⁴ (Pleyel Collection, Paris). This piano once belonged to Frédéric Chopin and it is said that he used it when composing many of his great piano works, including some of the Préludes, the G minor Nocturne, Op 37, No 1, the funeral march of the B minor Sonata, Op 34 and the F minor Fantasie Op 49, and that his last concert in February 1848 was played on this instrument.

PLATE 79
Joseph Joachim and Clara Schumann, 1854. Drawing by Adolph von Menzel, Germany, 1815–1905 (Staatsbibliothek, Berlin). Clara Schumann's favorite piano is said to have been one by Grotrian-Steinweg —the firm founded by Theodore Steinweg who remained in Germany when his father and brothers came to the United States to found the Steinway firm under their Americanized name. Here she is accompanying the famous violinist Joseph Joachim who performed often with Clara Schumann's lifelong friend, Johannes Brahms, at the piano.

PLATE 80

Upright piano by Pleyel, Paris, 1857–8; compass AAA to a⁴, two pedals: *una corda,* damper (Smithsonian Institution, 291,775, Hugo Worch Collection). Lavishly decorated in a manner derived from the masterpieces of André Charles Boulle, celebrated cabinet-maker of Louis XIV's time, this small upright piano is covered with tortoise-shell over a red ground. It has an ornate brass handle on each side and delicate candelabras with pale-pink glass shades. A few of the small pianos popular at this date were ornamented in this extravagant style.

PLATE 81

Young Girls at the Piano. Painting by Auguste Renoir, France, 1892 (The Lehman Collection, New York). The young French girls in this painting are pleasurably engaged in making music at a small piano of the type made popular by Pleyel. It recalls the one in the preceding plate.

6

EARLY MUSIC AND KEYBOARD INSTRUMENTS IN AMERICA

Some of this material has previously appeared in an article by this author in "The Piano, a Mirror of American Life" privately printed for members of the Schubert Club of St. Paul, Minnesota, and used by permission.

In the New World the beginnings of music, early keyboard instruments, and the rapid rise of piano manufacturing to a position of distinction by the mid nineteenth century constitute a typically American story.

The American colonists were as enthusiastic about music as their contemporaries in England, but they had fewer musical instruments and fewer hours of leisure. Coming from a country in which music played an important part in social life, it would be surprising if, in the new land, it was abandoned and forgotten and, indeed, it was not.

The Pilgrims, as they were departing for America, sang psalms, but there is no mention of their having taken musical instruments on board. While it is true that they frowned on the use of musical instruments in church, the myth that they opposed all instrumental music has long been dispelled. There are allusions to music in the writings of members of the Puritan community, and mention is made of music and singing at gatherings, "music" usually referring to instrumental music, but one can hope the singing was also musical. That there were exceptions even to the preclusion of instruments in church is suggested in a tract by John Cotton in 1647 entitled 'Singing of Psalms of Gospel Ordinance' that says 'nor do we forbid the use of any instrument of music there withall; so that attention to the instrument does not divert the heart from attention in the matter of song.'

Inventories of Boston and surrounding villages show 'a ould pair of virginals' listed as early as 1645. Since no instruments were being made in America at that time, so far as we know, it is significant that space was allowed on a small crowded sailing vessel to import even a virginal. The inventories of 1733 include thirteen virginals, two harpsichords, one spinet along with a clavichord, guitars, citterns (the English pear-shaped guitars), bass and treble viols, a chamber organ, flutes, bassoons, some 70 instruments in a population of about 13,000. These were found 'In the Paller, in Ye New Hall Chamber, in the closett in the Kitchin Chambr, in the Parlour, in Ye chamber over ye hall, in the Hall, in the North Chamber, in the little Chamber, in the Meale Chamber.'

An advertisement in a Boston newspaper of 1716[42] announced the arrival of various musical instruments and advertised tuning and stringing of virginalls (sic) and spinnets (sic). A few spinets were made on American soil by immigrants, German or English, and at least one of 1789 by native born Samuel Blythe.

The Moravians in Bethlehem, Pennsylvania, practiced music more seriously than any other group of 18th century Americans.[43] Centered around divine worship, the musical culture of the Moravians in Pennsylvania and the Carolinas was the most sophisticated to be found in the colonies. Gustav Hesselius of Philadelphia, a harpsichord maker, announced in 1775 'his extraordinary instrument by the name of pianoforte.' In the same city in the same year, we are told, John Behrent, a German immigrant living in Philadelphia, made the first piano in America.[44] David Tannenberg, the Moravian organ builder who made 'a kind of harpsichord' in Salem, North Carolina, in 1789 is said to have made several pianos, but none has survived so far as we know.

The diary of a Philadelphia belle, Nancy Shippen, gives a colorful picture of a gay social life with the glamorous young men of the French legation, the first established in the United States. She spent many evenings playing the harpsichord for her admirers—but never tells us what she played. Apparently the grace of a pretty young woman at the keyboard, rather than the music itself, beguiled the Frenchmen. In 1797, at fifteen, her talents were many; she could sing and play harpsichord and guitar, knew some French and many English poems and essays, could do every form of needlework, knew all the domestic arts such as pickling and preserving and clear starching. Naturally, she could curtsy and dance and conduct herself with elegance. All these accomplishments seemed to be of equal importance, and she was cautioned by her mother-in-law 'with respect to music it is a science which requires a life's practice to make a great proficiency in, and a girl of moderate fortune has many things much more useful to learn. A little music at the age of 12 or 14, sufficient to entertain herself and friends occasionally is, I think, quite sufficient.' This attitude toward young women performers was to prevail through much of the nineteenth century.

The Marquis de Chastellux, Major General of the French army during the Revolution recalling his visit to Philadelphia in 1780 wrote:

> In the afternoon we drank tea with Miss Shippen. This was the first time, since my arrival in America, that I had seen music introduced into society and mix with its amusements. Miss Rutledge sang with timidity but with a pretty voice . . . The Vicomte de Noailles took down a violin . . . and he made the ladies dance . . . When music, and the fine arts, come to prosper at Philadelphia, when society becomes easy and gay there, and they learn to accept of pleasure when it presents itself, without a formal invitation, then may foreigners enjoy all the advantages peculiar to their manners and government, without envying anything in Europe.

In Portsmouth, New Hampshire, with an affluent aristocracy, grown wealthy exporting lumber to the sugar islands and importing rum on the return voyages, there were more private carriages and liveried servants in proportion to the number of inhabitants than in any other place in New England. Judging from the number of announcements offering instruction to ladies and gentlemen on the harpsichord and other instruments, New Hampshire had, also, more than its share of musical instruments. In 1789 a number of instruments were advertised for sale in the 'New Hampshire Spy,' including a "fine toned" pianoforte. Tuning and repair services were also offered.

A domestic musical life flourished in the southern colonies, in which there were many settlers who had arrived before the voyage of the *Mayflower*. Most of them were cavaliers, younger sons who could not aspire to inherit the family estates and so decided to strike out on an adventurous life, hoping to establish estates of their own in the New World. Settling first in Virginia, then later the Carolinas and Maryland, these English noblemen and gentlemen had grown up in a tradition of music-making where the center of the world's musical culture in the 16th century was the court of Queen Elizabeth I, herself a virginalist of note. Life was more relaxed in the South than in New England. Virginians as a whole were devoted to the Church of England and the higher classes were not under the influence of the severe Puritan philosophy. Ladies and gentlemen played musical instruments as a matter of course, the ladies favoring keyboard instruments and the English guitar, the gentlemen the violin, German flute and horn. Music-making and dancing by family groups and with friends from neighboring plantations were a vital part of a lively, intimate social life. Itinerant music and dancing teachers were kept busy travelling from one plantation to another unless they were retained as resident tutors. It is claimed with ample justification that the Colonial South was richer in music than the New England colonies.

Colonel Carter, on his extensive plantation 'Nomini Hall,' had a fine large library of music and his family could make up a small orchestra. He could transpose on the flute and harpsichord and was probably the first American to acquire a piano. Philip Fithian, a Princeton theology student, engaged in 1773 and 1774 to tutor the Carter children, wrote in his memoirs that Colonel Carter often went without supper to entertain his guests by playing the Fortepiano while they supped.

Thomas Jefferson's musical activities are too well known to need emphasizing. His wife played keyboard instruments and guitar, and in 1771 he wrote to a London factor cancelling a previous order for a clavichord and requesting a piano. It is likely he had seen Colonel Carter's.

A German officer paroled and settled near Charlottesville in 1779 expressed, in a Hamburg newspaper, his admiration for Jefferson's skill on the violin and Martha's on the keyboard. Jefferson's library, as well as

Carter's, contained much music that was being played in England and on the Continent. While in Paris in 1774, he rented a piano for his daughter, Patsi.

Pianos were commonly known and used here when George Washington purchased an English harpsichord from the London firm of Longman and Broderip in 1793—probably the last to come to America and among the last made in England. It was for Nellie Custis, his step-granddaughter, and she was strongly encouraged to practice on it.

These random observations on music in early America—and they are just that, for music was practiced to some extent in virtually every colony—are intended to show that *hausmusik* was already a well established tradition in America when the piano was introduced.

The Colonists were ever anxious to emulate the modes and customs of the mother country, poring over fashion books to copy or to have copied the latest styles in dresses and bonnets, learning the latest dance steps brought by new settlers or visitors, seizing on every scrap of news of what was 'being done' in England. One would expect them, then, to long to acquire pianos when news of them reached these shores, but the speed with which they did so was truly remarkable. Since the harpsichord had been in use since the fourteenth century, it is astonishing how quickly the piano replaced it to satisfy the demands of a changing style of musical composition and performance.

We have seen that Colonel Carter was the first to own a piano. Only three years after he acquired it, the *New York Journal* carried an advertisement of salvaged cargo from the ship *Pedro* bound for Baltimore. Included were 'three hammer harpsichords (pianos) slightly damaged.' Among the seafaring merchants who brought over pianos was John Jacob Astor, who was exporting furs and, on the return journey, bringing back a large assortment of musical instruments, including pianos, made by his brother, George, in London. He set up shop for the sale of these 'on very low terms for cash' but soon turned his business over to others in order to devote his attention to more lucrative shipping, banking, and real estate activities. It is interesting to note that piano merchandising had a small place in the founding of one of America's great fortunes. A concert in which a piano, almost certainly an English import, was used, was held in New York as early as 1773.

The vogue for the piano increased rapidly, and in the last quarter of the century, the harpsichord was losing favor to the piano just as it was in England. The year 1800 found the harpsichord virtually obsolete.

It is estimated that in 1791[45] about twenty-seven Boston households contained pianos, all of them London-made. If one is to believe Jacques Pierrot Brissot de Warville, a distinguished French visitor to Boston, the music heard there was less than first rate. He wrote:

> In some houses you hear the forte piano. This art, it is true, is still in its infancy; but the young novices who exercise it are so gentle, so complaisant, and so modest that the proud perfection of art gives no pleasure equal to what they afford. God grant that the Bostonian women may never, like those of France, acquire malady of perfection in this art. It is never attained but at the expense of domestic virtues.

Although pianos were fairly common in the more comfortable households on the eastern seaboard by 1800, it is surprising to read in Chateaubriand's account of his travels in America in 1791, when he was 23 years old, that in the dwelling of a planter in the trackless wilds near Niagara he

> found . . . a delightful family, with all the charm and all the elegance of Europe—mahogany furniture, a piano, rugs, mirrors—all that four paces from the hut of an Iroquois. In the evening, when the servants had returned from the woods with an axe or a plow, the daughters of my host would sing the music of Paisiello and Cimarosa in sight of the wilderness and sometimes with the sound of the cataract in the background.

One suspects, however, that Chateaubriand, the founder of French romanticism, was romanticizing his memoirs not set down until thirty-six years after his travels. It is as unlikely that a piano was found so far west in 1791 as it is that the young ladies were singing the music of Paisiello and Cimarosa and that dancing lessons to the Indians paid for in beaver skins and bear hams were given by M. Violet, a French dancing master. The memoirs continue:

> In the midst of a forest . . . I found in this barn a score of savages, men and women, raven's feather on their heads and rings in their noses. A little Frenchman, powdered and curled as in the old days with an apple green coat, brocaded jacket, muslin frill and cuffs was scraping a miniature violin having the Iroquois dance 'Madelon Friquet' (popular air of the period). M. Violet . . . always said 'these gentlemen Savages and these lady Savages' . . . Holding his little violin between his chin and his chest (he) would tune up the fatal instrument; he would cry in Iroquois 'Places' and the whole troupe would jump like a band of demons.

Improbable as these events seem, however, Charles Maurice de Talleyrand in his memoirs of 1794 reported seeing a piano 'ornamented with the most beautiful bronzes' in a log cabin on the Ohio River. The owner apologized that the piano hadn't been tuned for a year.

Ladies, and especially young ladies, had a virtual monopoly on keyboard performance. Colonel Carter was a rare exception. Playing the harpsichord or piano was mainly in the hands, literally and figuratively, of the daughters of families. If they continued to play when they were mothers, we don't hear of it. This state of affairs continued well into the 19th century until, in fact, concert pianists began to make their appearance here. Arthur Loesser comments that 'feminine keyboard practice droops sharply after the mating season.' How often do we hear today the same apology offered by a nineteenth century lady who, when urged to play for her guests, demurred saying, 'Do excuse me, sir, I beg of you. I have not touched an instrument of music half a dozen times since I was married—one, you know, has so much to do.'

It was some years after the Revolution before the piano industry in America was well launched, but the early 19th century saw the establishment of a number of piano makers, many of them English or German, in Philadelphia, where Charles Albrecht had been making good instruments since at least 1789, and in New York, Boston, and Baltimore. These were acclaimed to have been 'made on the best London principles,' while London pianos were still being imported in great numbers. Indeed, American pianos were, at first, slavish copies of the English square pianos, but it was not long before American pianos were competing successfully with imported ones, and Americans began making innovations and improvements that gave their instruments a distinctive character leading ultimately to the piano of the mid-nineteenth century that revolutionized the industry. Native enterprise combined with the influence of experienced immigrants, especially from England and Germany, come to try their luck on American soil, led to the establishment of an extremely important industry. Piano makers proliferated astonishingly and soon every family with pretensions to culture, an interest in music and enough money to buy one was determined to have a piano in the parlor.

By 1785 pianos were commonly made in New York and about 1798 Benjamin Crehore founded the 'Boston school' of piano-makers in nearby Milton, Massachusetts. He had as apprentices Alpheus Babcock and John Osborn. Osborn in turn took James Stewart, a Scot, and Jonas Chickering of New Hampshire, into his own shop. All made important contributions to piano-making and their names will reappear later in this chapter.

Meanwhile, a number of makers from England and the Continent were coming to try their luck on American soil and from 1800 on American piano industry rapidly gained momentum. Native enterprise and ingenuity combined with the influence of the experienced foreigners contributed to its success.

As to the earliest American contribution to literature for the keyboard, Hopkinson's eight songs to be accompanied by harpsichord or piano are something of a milestone. They were engraved in Philadelphia in 1788, the first music involving harpsichord and piano to be published in this country. Hopkinson claimed to have been the first native of the United States to produce a musical composition; two of his earlier works date from 1754 and 1759.

JOHN HAWKINS AND THE UPRIGHT PIANO

Towards the end of the eighteenth century John Isaac Hawkins, a young English engineer with an inventive turn of mind,[46] emigrated to

Philadelphia and began to concern himself with innovations in piano construction, as his father had done in England. He patented several piano stops for novel effects, but most important was his design for an upright piano, the credit for the development of which he shares with Mathias Müller of Vienna, who brought out a similar instrument in precisely the same year, 1800. The vertical instrument of William Stodart and others (see plate 68) had been scarcely more than a conventional piano turned upright and placed on a stand. The Hawkins and Muller pianos utilized the space extending to the floor by running the strings vertically from top to bottom inside a surprisingly small rectangular case (as seen in plate 87). This stringing plan with the addition of over-stringing as well and also a front-to-back striking action applied to larger instruments created the type of upright piano without which, by the end of the nineteenth century, no American middle-class home was complete.

The Hawkins piano (plate 86) is noteworthy for a metal frame in which the soundboard is suspended and for a metal-covered wrestpin block—probably the first such use of metal. Although there is no evidence that Hawkins influenced other makers—his piano was in fact a failure as a musical instrument—his work reflects contemporary interest in experiments to solve the problems created by the increasing demands made on the piano.[47]

ALPHEUS BABCOCK

In 1825 Alpheus Babcock, a Boston maker who worked for a time in Philadelphia, produced a complete metal frame cast in one with the hitchpin block (plates 88, 89). Although Hawkins had already used iron bracing and Broadwood had made a piano in 1821 with two iron bars in the treble and one in 1825 with an iron frame under the soundboard, in general, resistance to iron framing had amounted almost to phobia. Its universal adoption at a later date, however, proved to be the answer to the problems that had been plaguing makers and performers.

Babcock deserves further credit for promoting the use of cross-stringing or over-stringing. Although the principle did not originate from him, his plan had far-reaching influence. It involved running the long bass strings diagonally above the others, so making more effective use of the available space. It can be seen in a later piano by Steinway (plate 94).

JONAS CHICKERING

The first great name in American piano-making is Jonas Chickering. In 1817 Chickering, 19-year-old-cabinet-maker's apprentice and son of a blacksmith and farmer in New Ipswich, New Hampshire, was summoned to make emergency repairs to a piano that had belonged to Princess

Amelia, youngest daughter of George III. The young man was musically inclined, could play fife and clarinet and had taught himself to read music, but he had had no experience in repairing musical instruments. Spurred by the challenge, however, he accomplished the task and, emboldened by his success, he set off not long after for Boston. After working for a year with a Boston cabinet-maker, he persuaded John Osborn, a leading piano-maker of the time, to hire him. Joinery, or cabinet-making, is solid training for the more esoteric craft of musical-instrument making—it has been the stepping-stone to such a career for many another—and the Osborn-Chickering association was fortuitous for both men.

In 1823, James Stewart, a young Scot who had been making pianos in Baltimore and Philadelphia, came to work in Osborn's shop but soon quarrelled with him and proposed that Chickering should join him in setting up their own shop. They worked together for three successful years before Stewart left for London to join the established firm of Collard & Collard, taking with him some of the Stewart-Chickering pianos, no doubt the first American pianos seen there. Stewart introduced a method of stringing used by the Boston makers and thereafter exchange of ideas between American and English makers was lively.

After a few years on his own Chickering again acquired a partner in John Mackay, a sea-captain and sharp businessman. Mackay set about making Chickering pianos known in the major cities of the United States and on voyages to South America took pianos with him, bringing back rosewood and mahogany for the shop. Mackay was lost at sea in 1841 but by this time the firm was on solid footing.

The problems of maintaining a wood-framed piano described earlier were occupying the attention of every maker. Babcock's metal frame for the square piano may have given Chickering the idea for an improved cast-iron frame that he patented in 1840 for the square piano and, in 1843, developed further for the grand model. These were the real 'breakthrough'. At the first International Exhibition held in the Crystal Palace in London in 1851, they created a sensation.

William Steinway hailed Chickering as 'the father of American pianoforte making'. Few would take issue with a more sweeping appellation: 'the father of the modern pianoforte'. A contemporary described him as 'upright, square and grand like his own pianos'. The piano shown in plate 91 incorporates the iron frame although it was made three years before Chickering took out his patent for it.

Chickering died prematurely in 1853, but not before he had started a gigantic new factory (the old one having been levelled by fire) and had taken his three sons as partners. The new plant, superbly planned and equipped, was said at the time to be the largest building on the continent apart from the United States Capitol. The sons were well educated, the concert in watching his feet from their front row seats. It transpired that they did not know the use of the pedals and saw in the movement of the feet a 'kind of queer trembling, and odd and rudimentary steps in dancing which, for two hours and a quarter, afforded them an inexhaustible source of amusement'.[48]

Although successful grands were being made in America by several manufacturers for some time, the demand for this model was limited and even affluent families inexplicably continued to acquire squares rather than emulate European taste for finer and more impressive grands (plate 92). By 1876 about one-sixth of the Steinway output consisted of grands and they made their last square in 1889—perhaps the last made in the United States. By 1900 the grand piano had become the accepted model for serious musicians and the concert stage and by 1904 square pianos had become such an embarassment to the industry that the manufacturers at their congress in Atlantic City acquired a number of them and ceremoniously set fire to them.

Meanwhile, uprights, already the prevalent economy model in Europe, had been replacing squares and the ubiquitous American reed organ that had enjoyed a vogue, especially in rural areas, as accompaniment for family and friendly groups singing hymns and popular ballads.

The first grand piano made in America was probably that of the Philadelphia firm of Loud Brothers. In 1826 they made an exceptional one for a Louisiana planter, a former New York cabbie made suddenly wealthy by the unexpected inheritance of a large fortune and plantation in Louisiana. Hoping to be accepted in society by impressing his not too cordial neighbors, he ordered an enormous grand, elaborately decorated and with a keyboard compass of seven and one-half octaves (the standard piano today has only seven and one-fourth). If it was the envy of all who saw it, it was a failure as a musical instrument and probably, also, as an entrée to society.

The rectangular piano called, unaccountably, square was the prevailing model in America through much of the 19th century. At first it was the graceful, lightly framed piano (plate 84), later a large heavy instrument (plate 93) into which was introduced, after 1840, a cast iron frame to withstand the heroic style of composition and performance of the romantic era. Americans were slow to take up the upright piano which by the mid-nineteenth century had replaced the square model abroad. The grand piano was relatively rare in private houses here until late in the century, even when the rest of the furnishings were opulent enough to suggest that the occupants lived in some degree of luxury in which a grand would be more appropriate (plate 92). Square pianos were made in inestimable numbers—hundreds of thousands—and every family with cultural pretensions found it necessary to have one. It became, in fact, a status symbol and family portraits often included the piano carefully painted and conspicuously present in the setting (cover illustration). Piano manufacturers and dealers proliferated. Itinerant peddlers and mail-order companies sold pianos, untried, to naive clients in the hinterlands to whom a piano was a piano without regard for quality. The manufacture of square pianos in America was discontinued by 1890, forty or fifty years after their demise in Europe, and the upright replaced it in modest homes.

Toward the end of the eighteenth century some piano-makers came under the spell of the fad for music of the Janissary guard of Turkish sovereigns. This military body had marched for several centuries to big drums, cymbals, triangles, and the Turkish crescent or 'Jingling Johnny', a pole to which were attached bells and crescents of metal to produce a rousing percussive din. The sound became so popular that other European rulers assembled in the eighteenth and nineteenth centuries their own 'Turkish' bands or introduced Turkish elements into their regimental bands. Mozart, Beethoven and others wrote worthy music in the Turkish style; some carried the idea even to the point of writing battle pieces with effects imitating the sound of cannons, clashing sabers, or galloping horses.

During some forty years of the nineteenth century, multiple pedals—as many as six—were attached to a considerable number of pianos of all shapes to imitate the Janissary sound. A typical arrangement of pedals, starting from left to right, is the following: (1) 'bassoon' which brings a roll of parchment into contact with the lowest three octaves causing a kind of buzzing sound; (2) a pedal operating a drum-stick that beats on the underside of the soundboard; (3) triangles and cymbals; (4) celeste soft pedal placing felt strips in front of hammers; (5) shifting *una corda* pedal; (6) damper pedal. The practice of adding bizarre effects was prolonged as piano transcriptions of orchestral works became popular.

The first patents for these gadgets were English, but European as well as American makers (plate 85) succumbed to them. The ultimate must have been a piano with chromatic kettledrums, patented in 1847 by Nunns & Fisher, New York.

The phenomenon described here is a debasement of the piano, mentioned only because it existed; it is best forgotten.

While the modern piano was being developed, a number of unsuccessful experiments were made. Most interesting among them was the Janko keyboard, which had no ultimate influence on the present-day piano, but reflected makers' concern with solving performance problems as well as the structural problems of the piano.

In 1882 Paul von Janko, a Hungarian musician and engineer patented a keyboard with six banks of short keys (plate 96). It was introduced by a Viennese piano-maker a few years later and in turn taken up by some American makers. Each row is tuned in the whole-tone scale: rows 1, 3, and 5 beginning with C; 2, 4, and 6 with C♯. The six rows constitute one keyboard operating on the same set of strings. Among the advantages attributed to it were that it compensated for the unequal lengths of the fingers, all diatonic scales could be played with only two sets of fingerings, and the octave span being smaller the hand could encompass a much greated stretch for widely spaced chords. The invention aroused some interest, claiming a few adherents, and a school was established in New York in 1891 to teach the method of playing it; but along with some other less well-conceived experiments, the Janko keyboard was abandoned after a few years. To the pianist whose ten fingers on occasions are either too many or too few, depending on the technical problem of the moment, multiple keyboards proved to be of no help.

Other experimental pianos worthy of passing notice were those with octave couplers on which a performer could play on one or another of the sets of strings or couple the two actions together much in the manner of the two manual harpsichords of earlier times. Erard Frères experimented in this direction in the early 1800s and in 1921 Emanuel Moor, a Hungarian-born pianist and inventor, brought out the Moor-Duplex piano with two keyboards an octave apart. Steinway, Bechstein, and Bösendorfer incorporated this mechanism into a few pianos and Moor's wife, the English pianist Winifred Christie, gave performances using the Moor keyboard in Europe and America. Interest in it waned with her disappearance from the concert scene.

American manufacturers willing to try anything to attract business in a highly competitive market, experimented with various kinds of novel musical instruments and at least one of them made a few so-called 'harp pianos' (plate 90). Omitting a soundboard, they stood the frame upright exposing its picturesque shape unenclosed by a case and provided it with a hammer action. It satisfied no demands.

For some time, musical composition and performance lagged, alas, behind the burgeoning piano-making industry. A writer in a Philadelphia periodical wrote in 1810:

> In no country of the world is the practice of music more universally extended, and at the same time the science so little understood as in America. Almost every house included between the Delaware and the Schuylkill has its piano or harpsichord, its violin, its flute or its clarinet. Almost every young lady and gentleman, from the Judge, the banker, and down to those of the constable, the huckster, and the drummer, can make a noise on some instrument or other and charm their neighbors with something which courtesy calls music. Europeans, as they walk through our streets, are often surprised with the flute rudely warbling 'Hail Columbia' from the oyster cellar, or the pianoforte thumped to a female voice screaming 'O Lady Fair!' from behind a heap of cheese, a basket of eggs, a flour barrel or a puncheon of apple whiskey; and on these grounds we take it for granted that we are a very musical people. Dr. Samuel Johnson made the snide but probably accurate remark that

'. . . In America the summit of attainment in that delightful science (music) seldom (reaches) higher than the accompanying of a song so as to set off a tolerable voice, or aid a weak one, and the attacting of a circle of beaus round a young lady, while she exhibits the nimbleness of her fingers in the execution of a darling waltz, or touches the hearts of the fond youths with a plaintive melody accompanied with false notes. Thus far, or but little further, does music extend, save in a few scattered instances.'

The rage for home-sung and home-played melodies stimulated a flood of music publishers at the turn of the century. Many titles were brought out, of which the majority were billed as 'simple songs for the piano'; that is, they were printed on two staves, the right hand a single line carrying the tune to aid the singer, the left a simple accompaniment. But as the performers became more accomplished, the publishers became more daring and brought out more elaborate versions on three staves, a publisher pointing out the obvious that a superior effect would be achieved by one who could sing one part while playing the other. Many of the songs were from current light operas and from collections of popular songs arriving from England. They were sweet or cute or both. Loesser entertained himself and his readers by listing a number of song titles beginning with 'sweet' or 'lovely': 'Sweet as Summer's Fragrant Gale,' 'Sweet is the Balmy Breath of Spring,' 'Lovely Nymph,' 'The Lovely Spring'—they go on and on.

There was a small minority of pianists playing the classics in their drawing rooms, but the great majority of keyboard playing was to accompany singing or dancing as in the cozy domestic scene in plate 92a. This state of affairs continued until Americans began to hear piano virtuosi from Europe. The first to arrive in 1845 was Leopold de Meyer, with a manager who waged a flamboyant press campaign. He, and better pianists who quickly followed, showed Americans how beautiful a piano well played could be and that a man could play the piano without losing his manhood or dignity. Since the first virtuosi heard here were foreigners, Americans began to feel that only in Europe, especially in Germany, could one learn to play the piano really well, and young hopeful pianists began to seek out teachers there. Even after fine schools of music were founded, such as Oberlin and Cincinnati Conservatories in 1867, followed shortly after by Chicago Musical College and New England Conservatory, European study was considered obligatory. Miss Amy Fay was probably the first American young lady to summon up the courage in 1869, to go to Germany for piano study, and her widely read letters, published in twenty editions before 1912, undoubtedly encouraged many another to follow her example. Although men by now were also inspired, women formed the great majority of piano students in Europe in the 70's and 80's. The American population in Berlin in 1891 was estimated at two thousand, most of them music students. If they all dreamed of glamorous careers in performance, most of them, then as now, had to settle for teaching, for playing for family friends to show off what they had achieved, or for arranging small private performances in churches, clubs, lodge halls or wherever an acceptable or even unacceptable piano was available. Their accomplishments, however, raised the quality of American musical life and revealed the joy of playing and hearing good piano music, either in private or in public.

The piano industry continued to flourish through the early years of this century and competition among makers was cut-throat. But then the tide began to turn in the late 1920's and piano sales fell to a low which proved disastrous to many small companies. Concerts involving pianos were more and more frequent, the number of good American pianists was growing, and the general level of taste was rising, while, strangely, the sale of pianos was diminishing. Perhaps for a time the market was saturated but even more important than the economic depression of the time was the competition from phonographs beginning in the 1910s, the introduction of radio broadcasting and the rush to buy sets in the 20s, and the player piano, at the height of its popularity in 1925.

An article in a periodical, *The Antiquarian,* in 1924 predicted gloomily:

> In the age of victrolas and radios, the piano is fast becoming a rare article in the ordinary home . . . Few persons now strum the abused instrument . . . The once ubiquitous instrument is now silenced, for only students of real talent are encouraged. The piano, therefore, is in danger of becoming as rare as a broughm, a phaeton or a dog cart for the banished horse.

An English visitor in 1925 concluded an article entitled, *The Passing of the Pianoforte* by saying, 'It would not surprise me if in another fifty years the piano were an extinct instrument along with the viol and the harpsichord.'

These harbingers of doom were dead wrong. In spite of the easy availability of fine recordings and the rage for television, today the piano market is again thriving more than fifty years later. The piano is still considered indispensable to general training in music; little boys and girls are still learning the piano, most of them with no ambition beyond providing pleasure to themselves and others in their own homes; more people play it in the United States than play all other instruments combined. Music schools are encouraging careers in music other than professional concert performance and emphasizing that music as literature can be as intellectually stimulating and soul-satisfying as the written word. Chamber music, with or without piano, for the sheer pleasure of musical communication and becoming familiar with the great literature, is attracting more performers of all degrees of proficiency.

While it is still rare to be entertained in a private house by piano music played by an amateur son or daughter in an informal concert or provided for dancing, there are many signs of a renewal of interest in simple music-making at home.

PLATE 82

At the Piano. Painting by James McNeill Whistler (1834–1903) (Taft Museum, Cincinnati, Ohio). In 1859 Whistler, in London on a visit from Paris, painted his half-sister, the wife of the well-known etcher and surgeon, Francis Seymour Haden. The little girl is her daughter. The family preoccupation with music is emphasized by the rapt attention of the figures at the piano and, further, by the inclusion of the cello case and what appears to be a violin case under the piano as part of the composition. Evidently the room was a setting for chamber music.

The large grand piano is unidentified as to maker, but it is probably a Broadwood, as the style of the legs and the carved keyboard are similar to those of some mid-nineteenth-century pianos by this firm.

PLATE 83 (*facing page, above*)

Square piano by Culliford, Rolfe and Barrow, London, c. 1790; compass FF to f³, two hand-stops: one for raising dampers from treble strings, the other from bass strings (Smithsonian Institution, 315,664, Hugo Worch Collection). This is typical of the pianos which were arriving in America in considerable numbers in the late eighteenth century. It is light in weight and can be easily lifted from its stand.

PLATE 84 (*facing page, below*)

Square piano by Charles Albrecht, Philadelphia, c. 1798; compass FF to f³, one hand-stop for raising the dampers (Smithsonian Institution, 288,399, Hugo Worch Collection). The influence of the English makers is reflected in the style of the case as well as in the mechanism.

PLATE 85

Square piano by A. Reuss, Cincinnati, Ohio, 1832–5; compass FF to f⁴, four pedals operating left to right as follows: bassoon stop, raises dampers, buff stop, bass drum and bells (Smithsonian Institution, 315,721, Hugo Worch Collection). The extraordinary pedal equipment of this early nineteenth-century piano is due to the fad that developed at the end of the eighteenth century for music of the Janissary, described on p95.

PLATE 86

Portable grand piano by John Isaac Hawkins, Philadelphia, 1801; compass FF to f³, two pedals: a Venetian swell and a buff stop (Smithsonian Institution, 313,619, Hugo Worch Collection). The keyboard of this piano folds up into a little portable cabinet with carrying handles on each side. Along with some new ideas (described pp90–1) incorporated into the structure of this piano, Hawkins revived some old ones. One pedal, instead of raising the dampers—as would be expected—operates a Venetian swell, a device invented by Burkat Shudi and used in the harpsichord in plate 50. Equally surprising is the reappearance of boxwood to cover the natural keys. It had been customarily used for this purpose in Italian harpsichords; the instruments in plates 27, 36 and 37 have boxwood naturals and ebony accidentals. Other woods and other materials such as tortoise shell and mother-of-pearl were sometimes chosen (see plate 47) and the keys of a few instruments were decorated with inlaid designs.

Ebony for naturals and bone for the tops of accidentals were commonly in use in France in the eighteenth century. Flemish seventeenth-century makers and the English were inclined to a reversal of this contrast and usually covered the naturals with bone or ivory and made the accidentals of ebony. The eighteenth-century Flemish harpsichord in plate 39, the French in plate 44, and the Stein piano in plate 57 all have ebony naturals and bone-capped accidentals. The spinet by Hitchcock in plate 38 has a stripe of ivory set into each ebony accidental, a favorite conceit of this maker. A few late nineteenth-century American heavy square pianos with elaborately carved and painted cases were fitted out with mother-of-pearl covered naturals.

The choice of material for keyboards seems to have been early a question of materials at hand and later one of individual preference, although the unlikely theory has been set forth that ebony naturals were selected for the purpose of showing off to advantage feminine white hands. In any event, around the beginning of the nineteenth century ivory naturals and ebony accidentals became standard; in recent years, however, a fine quality of plastic has been substituted for ivory.

Thomas Jefferson bought one of Hawkins' upright pianos for his Virginia mansion 'Monticello', but soon afterwards wrote to complain that it would not stay in tune even for an hour. Hawkins replied that he was not surprised, that he realized what the trouble was and could correct it if the piano were returned to him. Pecuniary embarrassment necessitated making a charge of $40 which he would repay after he arrived in England. Meanwhile Jefferson had read of Hawkins' new invention, the 'claviola', and thought he might like to trade the piano for one. Hawkins had no claviola available, however, and proposed exchanging the piano for another at a cost of $300 allowing for an original purchase price at $250. The correspondence does not reveal how all this was resolved.

The claviola deserves a word as an experimental keyboard instrument. Its keyboard compass is two octaves and two notes and it contains a perpendicular viol-shaped soundboard across which are stretched wire strings. In front a guide sliding along a brass rod holds a violin bow. On pressing a key the string is raised and brought in contact with the bow. Hawkins made extravagant claims for the beauty of its sounds. It recalls some experiments described earlier that were made with harpsichords in the seventeenth century.

These instruments of Hawkins were not successful musically, but they suggest contemporary interest in experimenting with novel keyboards.

PLATE 87
Interior view of the piano illustrated in the preceding plate.

PLATE 88 *(facing page, above)*
Square piano by Alpheus Babcock made at William Swift's Piano Forte
Manufactory, Philadelphia, c. 1835; compass FF to f⁴, two pedals: one
slides felt between hammers and strings, the other controls dampers
(Smithsonian Institution, 315,690, Hugo Worch Collection). This piano
has a complete metal frame cast in one piece—a revolutionary idea at the
time. The greater weight of the instrument with iron framing necessitates
increasing the size of the legs. Acceptance of the iron frame was slow, but

when it caught on, the graceful little square pianos with spindly legs such as those in plates 83 and 84 could no longer be made. A square piano can often be quite precisely dated simply on the basis of the style of its legs. Babcock has managed to design here an attractive piece of furniture, but some later makers, not so well endowed with taste, produced many square pianos supported by monstrously large and ugly legs.

PLATE 89
Plan view showing the tubular iron frame of the piano by Alpheus Babcock in the preceding plate.

PLATE 90
Harp piano, probably by Kuhn and Ridgeway, Baltimore, 1857; compass CC to c⁵, two pedals: *una corda,* damper (Smithsonian Institution, 299,854, Hugo Worch Collection). This experimental instrument had a very short life.

PLATE 91
Concert grand piano by Chickering, Boston, 1840; compass CC to c⁵, two pedals: *una corda,* damper (formerly Henry Ford Museum, Dearborn, Michigan). This piano with its handsome rosewood case is the first grand made by Chickering. It contains the successful cast-iron frame that he patented three years later.

PLATE 92

Mr and Mrs Ernest Fiedler and Family. Painting by Franz Heinrich, New York, c. 1846 (collection of Mrs William L. Rich, New York). In an opulent setting such as this, one would expect to find a grand piano, but the square model continued in favor in the United States for most of the nineteenth century long after it had been given up for the upright and grand models in England and on the continent.

PLATE 92a

The Dance, lithograph by Harry T. Peters. America, c. 19th century (Smithsonian Institution). Depicts a cozy domestic scene of dancing to the accompaniment of square piano.

PLATE 93
Square piano by Steinway & Sons, New York, 1877–8; compass AAA to
c⁵, two pedals: *una corda,* damper (Smithsonian Institution, 381,444,
Hugo Worch Collection). A piano of the type that made history at the
American Institute in 1855 and created a sensation at the Paris Exposition
of 1867.

PLATE 94
Plan view showing the full
iron plate and over-
stringing of the Steinway
piano in the previous plate.

Le public de l'exposition, saisit tout à coup de la rage de se faire pianiste à
l'audition des admirables pianos américains Steinway.

PLATE 95
Lithograph by Amédée de Noé ('Cham'), Paris, c. 1867 (collection Steinway & Sons). The Steinways applied the principles of iron framing and
over-stringing to the grand piano in 1859 and favorable articles about
their new piano appeared in European musical journals. The success of the
Steinway piano at the Paris Exposition of 1867 is recognized by this
cartoonist.

The caption reads in translation:

The public at the exposition is suddenly seized with the rage to become
pianist on hearing the admirable American Steinway pianos.

It will be noticed that the original lithograph was presented to the Steinways by the noted pianist, Vladimir Horowitz.

PLATE 97
Line drawing of the action of a modern grand piano. Well before the turn of the century the mechanism of the American piano had achieved its modern form in all essential details. It can be seen in this drawing that the action of a modern grand piano is an awesome feat of engineering containing nearly 12,000 individual parts. It was evolved over more than 200 years through the combined ingenuity, imagination and labor of numerous inventors and craftsmen.

DIAGRAM OF GRAND ACTION

1	Keybed	13	Key Stop Rail	25	Action Hanger	45	Drop Screw
2	Keyframe	14	Dag	26	Support Rail	46	Hammershank
3	Front Rail	15	Key	27	Support Flange	47	Knuckle
4	Front Rail Pin	16	Key Covering	28	Support	48	Hammer
5	Front Rail Pin Punching	17	Sharp	29	Support Cushion	49	Underlever Frame
6	Balance Rail	18	Front Pin Bushing	30	Fly	50	Underlever Frame Spring
7	Balance Rail Stud	19	Key Button	31	Tender	51	Underlever Frame Cushion
8	Balance Rail Pin	20	Balance Pin Bushing	32	Fly Regulating Screw	52	Underlever Flange
9	Balance Rail Bearing	21	Capstan Screw	33	Spoon	53	Underlever
10	Back Rail	22	Backcheck	34	Support Top Flange	54	Underlever Top Flange
11	Back Rail Cloth	23	Backcheck Wire	35	Balancier	55	Damper Wire Screw
12	Key Stop Rail Prop	24	Underlever Key Cushion	36	Balancier Regulating Screw	56	Tab
				37	Repetition Spring	57	Damper Stop Rail
				38	Repetition Felt	58	Damper Wire
				39	Balancier Covering	59	Damper Guide Rail
				40	Hammer Rest	60	Damper Head
				41	Regulating Rail	61	Damper Felts
				42	Letoff Regulating Screw	62	String
				43	Hammer Rail	63	Agraffe
				44	Hammershank Flange	64	Tuning Pin
						65	Sostenuto Rod

PLATE 98
Felt-covered hammers of a
modern grand piano,
tapered and graduated in
size as developed from Jean-
Henri Pape's ideas of 1839.

1　Bass Hammer

73　Treble Hammer

27　Treble Hammer

88　Treble Hammer

PLATE 99
(*caption overleaf*)

PLATE 99 (*preceding page, below*)

Frame of a modern concert grand. The cast-iron frame of a concert grand of today is built to withstand a tension of approximately 20 tons. The average tension of a single string is 165lb.

The diameters of the strings vary from approximately ⅓in (including the copper over-spinning around the steel core) for the lowest to 1/30in for the highest. The over-spinning or over-winding of the low strings was adopted as the keyboard compass was extended in order to lengthen the bass strings in correct proportion to the treble without making an impossibly long instrument. The lowest eight strings are single—one for each key—the next twelve are in pairs, and from there on up each hammer strikes three steel strings (Many early pianos were double-strung throughout.) The top twenty-one keys need no dampers, their vibrations being so small that it is unnecessary to subdue them.

The American concert grand is just under 9ft long. Bösendorfer of Austria makes, however, a grand that is 10ft long with a keyboard compass extended to eight octaves. All other keyboards remain at the compass adopted in the late nineteenth century: AAA to c^5 or seven octaves plus a minor third.

The advantages of the grand over the upright shape lie in several areas. The floor under the former acts as a secondary soundboard, and the raised lid projects the sound in the direction of the audience whereas the upright is designed to be placed against a wall which is by nature acoustically dead. The hammers and dampers of a grand fall by gravity obviating the spring mechanism required for the upright. It hardly needs to be added that the grand shape is aesthetically more pleasing and the position of the performer in relation to the audience is more satisfactory.

PLATE 100 (*facing page*)

Concert grand piano by Steinway & Sons, New York, 1903; compass AAA to c^5, three pedals: *una corda, sostenuto,* damper (on loan from the White House to the Smithsonian Institution, 379,287). This piano, the 100,000th made by Steinway, was presented to the United States government to commemorate fifty successful years of piano-making. It incorporates the metallic action frame patented in 1869, the repetition action, the *capo d'astro*[49] (or *capo tasto*) bar of 1875, the duplex scale of 1872 and the *sostenuto* pedal of 1874. This last, the middle or *sostenuto* pedal, here makes its only appearance in these illustrations. It was developed by Boisselot et Fils of Marseilles. When depressed with the left foot while one or more notes are struck, it permits these tones to continue sounding by immobilizing their raised dampers. At the same time other notes may be played and pedalled with the damper pedal as usual.

It was adopted by the Steinway firm in 1874, but it was never popular with European makers and was ignored or soon abandoned by them. It is seldom used and is considered a nuisance by some pianists. Josef Hoffman even had it removed from the pianos he used.

The case of the sumptuous piano illustrated here was designed by R. D. and J. H. Hunt. It is decorated with paintings by Thomas Dewing and with the seals of the original thirteen states on gold leaf background.

Its presence enhanced many a state occasion at the White House until it was replaced by the 300,000th Steinway made in 1938. It is now exhibited in the Smithsonian Institution in the First Ladies Hall.

7

STRINGED KEYBOARD
INSTRUMENTS TODAY

By the last quarter of the nineteenth century fine pianos were being made in many parts of the world. Among respected piano-makers in Germany were Bechstein, Blüthner, Grotrian-Steinweg;[50] in Austria Bösendorfer; in England Broadwood; in France Pleyel and Erard; in the United States Steinway, Chickering, Knabe, and Mason and Hamlin.

Iron framing, repetition action and tapered felt hammer covers were in universal use, and well before the turn of the century the keyboard compass of seven octaves plus a minor third (AAA to c⁵) became standard.

Many of these nineteenth-century instruments are still in use and are cherished for their distinctive tonal quality. But serious makers have not been content to rest on their laurels, and constant experimentation for the 'ideal' piano continues. In the 1930s the Steinway firm patented its 'accelerated action' which is faster and more responsive than its predecessors. More recently it has added the 'perma-free action' intended to make the instrument more stable and durable in all changes of climate. In the 1960s the Baldwin company set out to make 'the most beautiful concert grand piano in the world' and to this end altered the lengths, gauges and layout of the strings, redesigned the bridge, and devised new pins for anchoring the strings to the metal frame. Its new instrument is much admired.

In the United States the peak year of popularity of the piano was 1909 when 364,545 pianos were purchased. Later the talking machine, motion pictures, the radio and other new forms of diversion caused it to fall from favor for some years, and the economic depression of the early thirties put some American makers out of business. Chickering, Knabe, and Mason and Hamlin were absorbed by other firms that continued using their names.

The piano, however, has slowly resumed its place of honor. From 107,000 various sizes and models shipped from manufacturers in the United States in 1937 the number rose to 208,941 in 1965, the highest in recent years.

More than 21,000,000 people now play the piano in the United States alone—about the same number as the combined total of all other instrumentalists.[51] The all-purpose musical instrument, the piano, is still considered basic for general training in music.[52]

Western piano-makers continue to prosper, and in Japan, the Nippon Gakki company, which produced its first piano as early as 1887, makes today an admirable piano, the Yamaha, in an enormous plant. With assembly-line methods, this turns out yearly an astonishing number of pianos along with a variety of other products, motorcycles included.

Renewed interest in the harpsichord parallels piano improvements.

The Pleyel piano firm made a few harpsichords in the 1880s and exhibited one at the Paris Exposition of 1889. Early in this century Wanda Landowska was including in her piano recitals a piece or two played on one of these instruments. They were not entirely satisfactory but Madame Landowska felt more and more strongly that harpsichord music should be played on a harpsichord rather than on a piano. After visiting European museums to see old instruments she conferred with Pleyel's chief engineer who drew up many plans for a new harpsichord and finally hit upon one that suited her. In 1912 she introduced her first large Pleyel harpsichord at a Bach festival. It was not a copy of an eighteenth-century instrument but it offered a similar sound; her performances revealed again the charm and beauty of music played on the type of instrument for which it was composed.

In the late 1880s in Paris, Louis Diémer, too, revived interest in the harpsichord, using in concerts a harpsichord made by Pascal Taskin in 1769 and which had remained in the Taskin family. In 1882 the owners had had it restored by Louis Tomasini and it was subsequently used by the Erard firm for study and as the basic design for its new model.

Arnold Dolmetsch must also receive special notice. A distinguished musician, French born, who had learned piano-making in his father's factory, he emigrated to England and, with a scholarly approach to the study of early instruments, built in 1894 his first clavichord and in 1895 his first harpsichord. In 1905 he was invited by Chickering & Sons to work at its plant in Boston and during the next four years made about seventy-five harpsichords. From 1911 to 1914 he produced some harpsichords for Gaveau in Paris, finally returning to England where his stringed keyboard instruments, lutes and viols, as well as his studies in early performance practices, aroused interest and admiration. The English pianist Violet Woodhouse was persuaded to try the Dolmetsch instruments and for many years, from about 1913, had a devoted following for her performances on his harpsichords and clavichords. An American pupil of Dolmetsch, John Challis, after study of clavichord- and harpsichord-making, set up his own workshop in Ypsilanti, Michigan, in the early 1930s, moving later to Detroit and to New York. He revived American interest in these instruments.

In time two schools of twentieth-century harpsichord-makers developed; one group builds instruments using modern techniques and materials in the interest of producing an instrument more rugged in construction and easier to maintain, and adding pedals to effect quick changes of registration. The other group, aspiring to recreate as faithfully as possible the baroque sound, uses great historical instruments as models.

The English and German makers, on the whole, belong to the first group. Frank Hubbard and William Dowd in the United States and Martin Skowroneck of Bremen, Germany, are outstanding representatives of the second group, making extraordinarily beautiful harpsichords that compete fairly with carefully restored early instruments. Many discerning musicians are turning to such instruments for performing harpsichord music. A pianist who has played the great harpsichord literature on a fine harpsichord may not find it practical to abandon the piano, but it is more than likely that he will approach the music differently as a result of the experience.

Just as by the end of the eighteenth century the piano was recognized as not an improved harpsichord but a new instrument, now in the twentieth century the harpsichord has been rediscovered as an instrument *sui generis* that the piano does not truly supplant. There is a growing inclination to prefer the harpsichord for the music composed for it and to reserve the piano for piano music, and some modern composers are even exploring the use of the harpsichord for expressing contemporary ideas. Interest is being shown too in rediscovering the expressive potential of the clavichord.

The 18th century piano, also, is enjoying a revival for music of the classical period and many Viennese and English pianos are being restored and/or copied.

The piano itself has limitations that, if different from those of the harpsichord, are no less real. Like the harpsichord, however, it can be an eloquent and sensitive means of musical expression in the hands of a performer who accepts its limitations while fully exploiting its potentialities. Cristofori could not have dreamed of the subtleties of nuance and delicacy of control of the modern piano.

But what is the future of the piano? Some fine composers are now writing for the 'prepared' piano. For the performances of their compositions non-musical material such as paper, rubber bands, nuts and bolts, are applied to the strings (plate 101). The instrument is then played not only from the keyboard. The strings are plucked, struck with the hands or by other means, and the case itself is treated as a percussion instrument. The resulting sound is fascinating if not always 'musical' in the traditional sense.

It is not yet clear whether the prepared piano is a manifestation of dissatisfaction with the standard piano such as that for the harpsichord in the late eighteenth century, that will result in a totally new keyboard instrument, or whether it is a passing fad like the Janissary pedals.

In another direction increasing experimentation by serious musicians with electronic music arouses speculation that the piano as a basic instrument will become obsolete. Some feel that musical development in the future lies in the direction of quarter tones or even smaller fractions.

Future keyboard instruments may have split keys to produce an increased number of tones within the octave like some seventeenth-century harpsichords (plate 36) and the piano by Johannes Zumpe mentioned on page 68. A few quarter-tone pianos made in Europe and the United States in the late nineteenth and early twentieth centuries have not received wide notice.

In the unlikely event of the piano being threatened by obsolescence, it is safe to assume, judging from the past, that makers will produce a new keyboard instrument or a major alteration of an existing type. So far, makers have risen successfully to challenges from composers and performers. At present, it appears that the piano is here to stay.

Prepared piano preparation chart. The leftmost "TONE" column is a musical staff (with **16va** and **8va** octave brackets and, at the bottom, bass-clef notes marked "8va bass" and "16va bass"). The rightmost "TONE" column gives pitch letter names.

Left-hand annotation near the 8va bracket: (DAMPER TO BRIDGE = 4 7/16; ADJUST ACCORDINGLY)

MATERIAL	STRINGS LEFT TO RIGHT	DISTANCE FROM DAMPER (INCHES)	MATERIAL	STRINGS LEFT TO RIGHT	DISTANCE FROM DAMPER (INCHES)	MATERIAL	STRINGS LEFT TO RIGHT	DISTANCE FROM DAMPER (INCHES)	TONE
			SCREW	2-3	1¼*				A
			MED. BOLT	2-3	1⅜*				G
			SCREW	2-3	1⅝*				F
			SCREW	2-3	1 13/16*				E
			SCREW	2-3	1¾*				E♭
			SM. BOLT	2-3	2*				D
			SCREW	2-3	1 9/16*				C#
			FURNITURE BOLT	2-3	2 3/16*				C
			SCREW	2-3	2½*				B
			SCREW	2-3	1⅞*				B♭
			MED. BOLT	2-3	2⅞*				A
			SCREW	2-3	2¼*				A♭
			SCREW	2-3	3¾*				G
			SCREW	2-3	2 5/16*				F#
SCREW	1-2	¾*	FURN. BOLT + 2 NUTS	2-3	2⅜*	SCREW + 2 NUTS	2-3	3¼*	F
			SCREW	2-3	1 9/16*				E
			FURNITURE BOLT	2-3	1⅞				E♭
			SCREW	2-3	1 15/16				E
			SCREW	2-3	1 1/16				C#
			MED. BOLT	2-3	3¾				C
			SCREW	2-3	4 7/16				B
RUBBER	1-2-3	4½	FURNITURE BOLT	2-3	1¼				A
			SCREW	2-3	1¾				G#
			SCREW	2-3	2 5/16				F#
RUBBER	1-2-3	5¾							F
RUBBER	1-2-3	6½	FURN. BOLT + NUT	2-3	6⅞				E
			FURNITURE BOLT	2-3	2 9/16				E♭
RUBBER	1-2-3	3⅝							D
			BOLT	2-3	7⅛				D♭
			BOLT	2-3	2				C
SCREW	1-2	10	SCREW	2-3	1	RUBBER	1-2-3	8¼	B
(PLASTIC (see G))	1-2-3	2 5/16				RUBBER	1-2-3	4½	B♭
PLASTIC (over 1 under 2-3)	1-2-3	2⅞				RUBBER	1-2-3	10⅛	G#
(PLASTIC (see D))	1-2-3	4¼				RUBBER	1-2-3	5 5/16	G
PLASTIC (over 1- under 2-3)	1-2-3	4⅛				RUBBER	1-2-3	9¾	D#
BOLT	1-2	15½	BOLT	2-3	11/16	RUBBER	1-2-3	14⅛	D
BOLT	1-2	14½	BOLT	2-3	⅞	RUBBER	1-2-3	6½	D♭
BOLT	1-2	14¾	BOLT	2-3	9/16	RUBBER	1-2-3	14	C
RUBBER	1-2-3	9½	MED. BOLT	2-3	10⅛				B
SCREW	1-2	5⅞	LG. BOLT	2-3	5⅞				B♭
BOLT	1-2	7⅞	MED. BOLT	2-3	2¼	SCREW + NUTS	1-2	1	A
LONG BOLT	1-2	8¾	LG. BOLT	2-3	3¼	RUBBER	1-2-3	4⅛	A♭
			BOLT	2-3	11/16				G
SCREW + RUBBER	1-2	4 7/16							D
ERASER (over D, under C# + E)	1	6¾							D

AM. PENCIL CO. #596

*MEASURE FROM BRIDGE.

NOTES AND REFERENCES

1 Patricia Egan. 'Concert Scenes in Musical Paintings of the Italian Renaissance', *Journal of the American Musicological Society*, vol XIV, no 2 (Richmond, Va: William Byrd, summer 1961).

2 Representations of the early clavichord are known in Italian, German, Dutch, English, French and Yugoslavian works of art.

3 1428 is the date given by several respected authorities, although slightly later dates are assigned by some others. 1433 is the latest reasonable date offered.

4 Personal letter from Konrad Marwinski.

5 Edwin M. Ripin. 'The Early Clavichord', *The Musical Quarterly*, vol LIII (1967), 531–5. The technical matter of the difference in construction of the early and later clavichords would have no appropriate place here but for the interesting representations of the early type. The student of the subject will wish to refer to Mr Ripin's excellent article.

6 Italian: *clavicembalo, gravicembalo, cembalo, spinetta;* French: *clavecin, espinette, épinette;* German: *Cembalo, Kielflügel.*

7 The practice of designating pitches as 8′, 4′, 16′, 2′ is carried over from organ terminology. The 8′ pipe of the organ sounds C, the 4′ sounds c, the 16′ CC, and the 2′ c′. See further explanation of pitch indications below:

AAA, BBB, CC, BB, C , B, c , b   c¹ b¹ c² b² c³ b³ c⁴   b⁴ c⁵

8 Also *eschiquier, eschaquier d'Angleterre* and in Spanish, *exaquier.*

9 *Les Traités d'Henri Arnault de Zwolle,* Bibliothèque Nationale MS BN Latin 7295. Facsimile edition, trans and ed by G. le Cerf and E. R. Labande (Paris: Edition August Picard, 1932), fol 128 ro, 5 (author's English translation).

10 Le Cerf and Labande. Introduction to *Les Traités d'Henri Arnault de Zwolle.*

11 Rosamond E. M. Harding. *The Piano-forte—Its History Traced to the Great Exhibition of 1851* (Cambridge, England: Cambridge University Press, 1933), p8, note 1.

12 *Les Traités d'Henri Arnault de Zwolle.*

13 Opinions on the date and provenance are those of Mrs Elizabeth P. Wells, Curator of Instruments, Royal College of Music, London.

14 *Basso continuo:* see p48.

15 Facsimile edition (Kassel, Germany: Bärenreiter, 1966), vol 4, pp634–43.

16 Frank Hubbard. *Three Centuries of Harpsichord Making* (Cambridge, Mass: Harvard University Press, 1965), p105.

17 Figured bass: see p48.

18 Maffei mistakenly wrote the name as Cristofali.

19 Fabbri, Mario. 'Il primo "pianoforte" di Bartolomeo Cristofori', *Chigiana Rassegna Annuale di Studi Musicologici,* vol XXI ns I, 1960 (Florence, Italy: Olschki, 1964), 162–72.

20 E. F. Rimbault, trans. *The Pianoforte* (London: Robert Cocks 1860), p99.

21 Ralph Kirkpatrick. *Domenico Scarlatti* (Princeton, New Jersey: Princeton University Press, 1953), chap IX, pp178–85.

22 Abraham Rees, ed. 'Ravalement', *Cyclopaedia* (London: Longman, Hurst, Rees, Orme and Brom, c. 1805–19).

23. Emily Anderson, ed and trans. *The Letters of Mozart and His Family* (London: Macmillan, 1966).

24 Dénes Bartha, ed. *Joseph Haydn Gesammelte Briefe und Aufzeichnungen* (Kassel, Germany: Bärenreiter, 1965) (author's translation).

25 Compare with a Zumpe piano of 1767 in the Victoria & Albert Museum, London (W 27–1958).

26 The Mozart household contained several pianos by Fritz Späth of Regensburg.

27 Emily Anderson, ed and trans. Op cit.

28 Some American orchestras now tune to 442 and others in Europe as high as 456.

29 Harding. Op cit, appendix C, p317 and following.

30 Edouard Ganche. *Frédéric Chopin, sa vie et ses oeuvres,* p351 (author's translation).

31 Ibid.

32 Arthur Loesser. *Men, Women and Pianos* (New York: Simon & Schuster, 1954).

33 Ibid, p410.

34 Frank Hubbard with exquisite logic called the keyboard with more than twelve notes to the octave 'nonenharmonic'; the term 'enharmonic' is customarily used.

35 Equal temperament was not universally adopted in Germany until c. 1800, in France and England c. 1850. It should be added that there are those who lament the abandonment of mean-tone temperament and a few are readopting it for the performance of early music. See John W. Link, Jr, 'The Promise of Meantone', *The Diapason* (January 1968).

36 Joseph Merlin was a Belgian inventor of extraordinary versatility. Among his inventions were a shorthand music-recording device attached to a harpsichord, a combined harpsichord and piano, a self-propelled invalid's chair, a pedal-operated tea table which caused the cups to rotate before the hostess, and roller skates.

37 Burney's six-octave piano has disappeared along with the harpsichord he mentions, but two other six-octave pianos by Merlin were still preserved in 1933 in England in the collection of Sir Albert Richardson.

38 F. C. Morse. *Furniture of the Olden Time* (New York: Macmillan, 1902), p262.

39 Harding. Op cit, appendix.

40 Personal letter from André Maurois, biographer of Hugo.

41 Author's translation.

42 Percy A. Scholes. *The Puritans and Music in England and New England* (New York: Russel & Russel, Inc, 1962), p36.

43 Pennsylvania Chapter of the Society of the Colonial Dames of America. *Church Music and Musical Life in Pennsylvania in the Eighteenth Century* (Lancaster, Pennsylvania: Wickersham Printing Co, 1926–47).

44 Daniel Spillane. *The History of the American Pianoforte* (New York: D. Spillane, 1790), p49.

45 Ibid, p76.

46 Hawkins was not only concerned with musical instruments; he was an indefatigable inventor. He once set up a short railway in Regent's Park, London, involving a railway, a carriage and horse and a differential pulley to demonstrate that with the aid of the pulley a horse could propel the carriage ten times as far as he moved. With Charles Wilson Peale, Hawkins patented a 'physiognatrace', capable of setting down on paper the outline of a person.

47 Four other such pianos by Hawkins are presently known.

48 Louis Moreau Gottschalk. *Notes of a Pianist* (London: J. B. Lippincott, 1881).

49 The *capo d'astro* (or *capo tasto*) bar, like the agraffe, is for the purpose of securing the down-bearing of the bridge on the soundboard and for preventing the strings from being knocked out of position by the hammers.

50 Founded by the son of Heinrich Engelhard Steinweg (Steinway), who stayed behind in Germany when the rest of the family came to the United States.

51 Statistics above provided by Steinway & Sons.

52 Even in Communist China in 1968 a piano was substituted for the first time for traditional gongs, cymbals and drums in a performance in Peking of the Chinese drama, *The Red Lantern*. Its use and the composition of the music for it were authorized, astonishingly and incongruously, by the Cultural Revolutionary Committee which issued the statement that the advantage of the piano is 'its wide range, its magnificent force and its varied ways of expression' that can bring into play 'the lofty and heroic images of the opera's characters'. The event *per se* is hardly of musical importance but it is striking evidence of the all-purpose nature of the piano and its continuing pervasion.

SELECTIVE BIBLIOGRAPHY

Anderson, Emily (trans). *The Letters of Mozart and His Family*. London: Macmillan, 1966

Apel, Willi. *Harvard Dictionary of Music*. Cambridge, Mass: Harvard University Press, 1962; rev and enlgd ed 1969

Arnault de Zwolle, Henri. *Instruments de musique du XVe siècle*. MS Fonds Latin 7295, Bibliothèque Nationale, Paris (Trans and ed G. Le Cerf and E. R. Labande. Paris: Editions Picard, 1932)

Bach, C. P. E. *Essay on the True Art of Playing Keyboard Instruments*, trans and ed William J. Mitchell. New York: W. W. Norton, 1949

Badura-Skoda, Eva. 'Prolegomena to a History of The Viennese Fortepiano.' *Israel Studies in Musicology*. Vol II, Israel Musicology Society, Jerusalem, 1980

Bédos de Celles, Dom François. *L'art du facteur d'orgues*, vol I. Paris: 1766 (Facsimile edition, Kassel, Germany: Bärenreiter, 1963)

Bessaraboff, Nicholas. *Ancient European Musical Instruments*. Cambridge, Mass: Harvard University Press, 1941

Boalch, Donald H. *Makers of the Harpsichord and Clavichord*. London: George Ronald, 1956

Bragard, Professor R. and DeHen, Dr Ferd J. *Les instruments de musique dans l'art et l'histoire*. Paris: Société Française du Livre, 1967. (Trans Bill Hopkins. *Musical Instruments in Art and History*. New York: Viking Press, 1968)

Brinsmead, Edgar. *The History of the Pianoforte with an Account of Ancient Music and Musical Instruments*. London, Paris and New York: Cassell, Petter & Galpin, 1877

Brown, Howard Mayer. *Instrumental Music Printed Before 1600*. Cambridge, Mass: Harvard University Press, 1965

Bruni, Antonio Bartolommeo. *Un inventaire sous la terreur. Etat des instruments de musique relevé chez les émigrés et les condamnés*, ed J. Galay. Paris: G. Chamerot, 1890

Buchner, Dr Alexander. *Musical Instruments through the Ages*, trans Iris Urwin. London: Spring Books, nd

Bukofzer, Manfred F. *Music in the Baroque Era*. New York: W. W. Norton, 1955

Bullock, Helen. *On Music in Colonial Williamsburg*. Williamsburg, Va: Dept of Research and Record, 1938

Chase, Gilbert. *America's Music*. New York: McGraw-Hill, 1955

Clemencic, René. *Old Musical Instruments*, trans David Hermges. New York: G. Putnam, 1968

Closson, Ernest. *History of the Piano*, trans Delano Ames. London: Paul Elek, 1947

Clutton, Cecil. 'The Pianoforte', *Musical Instruments through the Ages*, ed Anthony Baines. Baltimore: Pelican Books, 1969

Colt, C. F. with Antony Miall. *The Early Piano* Stainer & Bell. London, 1981

Couperin, François. *L'art de toucher le clavecin*. Paris, 1717. (Reissued with English and German trans Leipzig: Breitkopf & Härtel, 1933)

———. *Pièces de clavecin*. Paris: Chez l'auteur, le sieur Foucaut, 1713–30

Dale, William. *Tschudi, the Harpsichord Maker*. London: Constable, 1913

Dart, Thurston. 'The Clavichord', *Musical Instruments through the Ages*, ed Anthony Baines. Baltimore: Pelican Books, 1969

David, Hans T. and Mendel, Arthur, eds. *The Bach Reader*. New York: W. W. Norton, 1945

Die Musik in Gerschichte and Gegenwart, ed Friedrich Blume. Kassel, Germany: Bärenreiter, 1949–66

Dolge, Alfred. *Pianos and Their Makers*. Covina, Calif: Covina Publishing Company, 1911, and New York: Dover Books, 1972

Donington, Robert. *The Interpretation of Early Music*. New York: St Martins Press, 1963

Dufourg, Norbert, ed. *La Musique*. Paris: Larousse, 1965

Encyclopaedia Britannica. 11th ed, ed Hugh Chisholm. Cambridge, England: Cambridge University Press, 1910

Fabbri, Mario. 'Il primo "pianoforte" di Bartolomeo Cristofori', *Chigiana Rassegna Annale di Studi Musicologici*, vol XXI, ns I. Florence, Italy: Olschki, 1964

Fay, Amy. *Music Study in Germany in the Nineteenth Century*. New York: Dover, 1965

Fithian, Philip Vickers. *The Journal and Letters of Philip Vickers Fithian*, ed and intro Hunter Dickinson Farish. Williamsburg, Va: Colonial Williamsburg, 1957

Fuller, David. 'Clavecin et Fortepiano au XVIIIe Siecle'. *Program notes for the Festival du Marais*, 1978, Paris.

Gaines, James R., Ed. *The Lives of the Piano*. New York: Holt, Rinehart, and Winston, 1981

Galpin, Francis W. *Old Instruments of Music*. London: Methuen, 1910

Ganche, Edouard. *Frédéric Chopin, sa vie et ses oeuvres*. Paris: Mercure de France, 1921

Geiringer, Karl. *Haydn: A Creative Life in Music*. Berkeley, Calif: University of California Press, 1968

Gill, Dominic, Ed. *The Book of the Piano*. Oxford: Phaidon Press, 1981

Goodwin, Mary. *Musical Instruments in Eighteenth Century Virginia*. Williamsburg, Va: Institute of Early American History and Culture, 1953

Gottschalk, Louis Moreau. *Notes of a Pianist*. London: J. P. Lippincott, 1881

Grove's Dictionary of Music, ed Eric Blom. 5th ed New York: St Martin's Press, 1959

Haake, Walter. *Am Klavier*. Königstein im Taunus, Germany: Hans Köster, 1968

Halfpenny, Eric. 'Music and Musical Instruments', *The Connoisseur Period Guide: The Georgian Period*. New York: Reynal, 1957

Hamilton, Clarence G. *Piano Music, Its Composers and Characteristics*. Boston: Oliver Ditson, 1925

Hanks, Sarah E. 'Pantaleon's Pantalon, an 18th Century Musical Fashion', The Musical Quarterly, vol LV, no 2. New York: G. Schirmer, April 1969

Harding, Rosamond E. M. *The Piano-forte—Its History Traced to the Great Exhibition of 1851*. Cambridge, England: Cambridge University Press, 1933. Reprinted New York: Da Capo Press, 1973

Harris, William Laurel. 'Musical Instruments as an Indication of Refinement and Culture', *Good Furniture*, vols VIII and IX. Grand Rapids, Michigan: Dean Hicks, January and July 1916

Harrison, Frank and Rimmer, Joan. *European Musical Instruments*. New York: W. W. Norton, 1964

Haydn, Joseph. *Gesammelte Briefe und Aufzeichnungen,* ed Dénes Bartha. Kassel, Germany: Bärenreiter, 1965

Hess, Albert G. 'The Transition from Harpsichord to Piano', *Gapin Society Journal,* vol VI. London: July 1953

Hipkins, A. J. *A Descriptive History of the Pianoforte.* London: Novello Ewer, 1896

Hirt, Franz Joseph. *Meisterwerke des Klavierbaus.* Olten, Switzerland: Im Urs Graf-Verlag, 1955

Hollis, Helen Rice. 'The Musical Instruments of Joseph Haydn' Smithsonian Institution Press, 1976

———. 'Jonas Chickering—The father of American pianoforte making' The Magazine *Antiques,* August 1973

———. *An Introduction to the Smithsonian Institution's Collection of Pianos,* Smithsonian Institution Press, 1973. Revised, 1974

———. 'The Domestic Piano in America' *The Piano—a Mirror of American Life.* The Schubert Club Keyboard Collection, St Paul, Minnesota, 1981

Hoover, Cynthia A. *Harpsichords and Clavichords.* Smithsonian Institution Press, 1969

Howard, John Tasker. *The Music of George Washington's Time.* Washington DC: George Washington Bicentennial Commission, 1931

———. *Our American Music.* New York: Thomas Y. Crowell, 1965

Hubbard, Frank. *Three Centuries of Harpsichord Making.* Cambridge, Mass: Harvard University Press, 1965

James, Philip. *Early Keyboard Instruments.* New York: Frederick A. Stokes, 1930

Juramie, Ghislaine. *Histoire du piano.* Paris: Prisina, 1947

Kirkpatrick, Ralph. *Domenico Scarlatti.* Princeton, NJ: Princeton University Press, 1953

Krehbiel, Henry Edward. *The Pianoforte and Its Music.* New York: Scribner, 1911

Lambert, Barbara. 'The Musical Puritans' *Old Time New England,* Boston, Winter, 1972

Lesure, François. *Musik and Gesellschaft im Bild.* Kassel, Basel, Paris, London, New York: Bärenreiter, 1966. (Trans Denis and Sheila Stevens. *Music in Art and Society.* Philadelphia: Philadelphia State University Press, 1968)

Link, John W., Jr. 'The Promise of Meantone', *The Diapason.* Chicago, 1968

Loesser, Arthur. *Men, Women and Pianos.* New York: Simon & Schuster, 1954

Marcuse, Sibyl. *Musical Instruments: A Comprehensive Dictionary.* Garden City, New York: Doubleday, 1964

———. 'Transposing Keyboards on Extant Flemish Harpsichords', *The Musical Quarterly.* New York: G. Schirmer, July 1952

Meer, van der, John Henry. 'Beiträge zum Cembalobau in Deutschen Sprachgebiet bis 1700', *Anzeiger des Germanischen Nationalmuseums,* 1966

———. 'Review of Three Centuries of Harpsichord Making by Frank Hubbard', *Journal of the American Musicological Society,* vol XX, no 1 (spring 1967), 143–6

Mersenne, Marin. *Harmonie Universelle.* Facsimile edition. Paris: Centre National de la Recherche Scientifique, 1963

Morse, F. C. *Furniture of the Olden Times,* New York: Macmillan, 1902

Newman, William S. 'Beethoven's Piano versus His Piano Ideals', *Journal of the American Musicological Society,* vol XXIII, no 3 (autumn 1970), 484–504

Parrish, Carl. *The Early Piano and Its Influence on Keyboard Technique and Composition.* Harvard University thesis, 1939. Superior, Wis: Research Microfilm Publications, 1953

Pennsylvania Chapter of The Society of the Colonial Dames of America. *Church Music and Musical Life in Pennsylvania in the Eighteenth Century.* Lancaster, Pennsylvania: Wickersham Printing Co, 1926–47

Pepys, Samuel. *Diary and Correspondence of Samuel Pepys,* ed Rev Mynors Bright. New York: G. E. Croscup, 1892

The Piano; a Mirror of American Life—various authors. The Schubert Club Keyboard Instrument Collection, St. Paul, Minnesota, 1981

Pirro, André. *Les Clavicinistes.* Paris: Laurens, 1925

Pols, André M. *De Ruckers en De Klavierbouw in Vlaandern.* Antwerp: N. V. De Nederlansche, Roekhande, 1942

Rees, Abraham, ed. *The Cyclopaedia.* London: Longman, Hurst, Rees, Orme & Brown, 1819

Restout, Denise and Hawkins, Robert, eds. *Landowska on Music,* New York: Stein & Day, 1965

Reynvaan, Joos Verschuere. *Musykaal Kunst-Wordenboek.* Amsterdam, 1795

Rimbault, Edward B. *The Pianoforte.* London: Robert Cocks, 1860

Ripin, Edwin M. 'The Early Clavichord', *The Musical Quarterly,* vol LIII, no 4. New York: G. Schirmer, October 1967

———. 'The Two-Manual Harpsichord in Flanders Before 1650', *The Galpin Society Journal,* vol XXI. Chichester, Sussex: Phillimore, 1968

———. 'A Scottish Encyclopedist and the Piano Forte', *The Musical Quarterly,* vol LV, no 4. New York: G. Schirmer, October 1967

Russell, Raymond. *The Harpsichord and Clavichord.* London: Faber & Faber, 1959. Revised ed Howard Schott, New York: W. W. Norton, 1973

Sachs, Curt. *Das Klavier.* Berlin: J. Bard, 1923

———. *The History of Musical Instruments.* New York: W. W. Norton, 1940

Scholes, Percy A. *The Puritans and Music in England and New England.* New York: Russell & Russell, 1962

———. *The Great Dr Burney.* London: Oxford University Press, 1948

———. *The Oxford Companion to Music.* London: Oxford University Press, 1938

Shortridge, John D. *Italian Harpsichord Building in the 16th and 17th Centuries.* Washington DC: US National Museum Bulletin, no 225, 1960; rev ed 1970

Sitwell, Sacheverell. *Baroque and Rococo.* New York: G. Putnam, 1967

Spillane, Daniel. *History of the American Pianoforte.* New York: D. Spillane, 1890

Steinert, Morris. *Reminiscences of Morris Steinert,* comp and ed Jane Marlin. New York and London: G. Putnam, 1900

Straeten, Edmond van der. *La musique aux pays-bas avant le XIXe siècle.* Ghent, Belgium: A. et F. Mahillon, 1867–88

Strunk, Olive, ed. *Source Readings in Music History.* New York: W. W. Norton, 1950

Sumner, W. L. *The Pianoforte.* London: MacDonald, 1966

Thayer, Alexander Wheelock. *The Life of Ludwig van Beethoven,* trans and ed H. E. Krehbiel, New York: The Beethoven Association, 1921–5

University of Edinburgh Faculty of Music. *The Russell Collection of Early Keyboard Instruments.* Edinburgh: University of Edinburgh, 1968

Virdung, Sebastian. *Musica Getutscht.* Basle: 1511. (Facsimile reprint, Berlin: Rob Eitner, 1882)

Winternitz, Emanuel. 'The Visual Arts as a Source for the Historian of Music', offprint from vol 1, *IMS Congress Report.* Kassel, Basle, London, New York: Bärenreiter, 1961

INDEX